CAN A NATION BE CHANGED IN A DAY?

How to Transform

Our Cities

for True Reformation

Amanda Wells

DESTINY IMAGE EUROPE
Via Maiella, 1
66020 San Giovanni Teatino (Ch) - Italy

ISBN: 88-89127-11-2

1 2 3 4 5 6 7 8/10 09 08 07 06 05

This book and all other Destiny Image Europe books are available at Christian bookstores and distributors worldwide.

To order products, or for any other correspondence:

DESTINY IMAGE EUROPE
Via Acquacorrente, 6
65123 - Pescara - Italy
Tel. +39 085 4716623 - Fax: +39 085 4716622
E-mail: info@eurodestinyimage.com

Or reach us on the Internet:

www.eurodestinyimage.com

Acknowledgements

To Jesus, my Lord—my eternal thanks to You will never be enough; I will forever be "Daddy's girl." My relationship with You grows every day. When life was hard, You were there. When others gave up on me, You were there. I will always love You.

To the silent heroes in a war unseen—thank you for defending the freedom, beliefs, and values that our nations were built upon. Some of you paid the price with your lives.

To Roger—thank you for your love, support, understanding, and the many TV dinners, without which this never would have been possible. After 27 years of marriage, I am still so in love!

To our children—for encouraging me, loving me, and releasing me to do His will and purpose for my life—you're the best! Thanks for your input. This book is because of and for you.

To my publisher, Pietro Evangelista, and his wife, Sandra—for believing in me and encouraging me! I consider you more than colleagues; I consider you my dear, close friends. Thank you.

To my "family" in the offices of Destiny Image Europe—thank you for all your hard labor, which is appreciated.

To Don Nori—who believed in me, and said, "You can do it!"

To Iverna Tompkins and the team of girls—you have been like a mother to me; thank you for your love, support, and wisdom that I have treasured so much.

To Stewart and Jane Moncreiff, our pastors—who are the most encouraging couple I have ever been privileged to know. You have an ability to draw out the best in us.

To all at COC Gold Coast—Thanks!!!

To all our friends and colleagues—there are too many to name—your support has been rich in love and has helped me to fulfill my purpose and destiny. Thanks.

Contents

"How do geese know when to fly to the sun?

Who tells them the seasons?

How do we, humans, know when it is time to move on?

As with migrant birds, so surely with us,

there is a voice within, if only we would listen to it,

that tells us so certainly when to go forth into the unknown."

—*Elisabeth Kubler-Ross*

*Even the stork in the sky knows her seasons; and the turtledove
and the swift and the thrush observe the time of their migration;
but My people do not know the ordinance of the Lord*

(Jeremiah 8:7 NAS).

Foreword

Amanda Wells has written this book with the same passion that she lives her life. She is never content to be just another follower of Jesus Christ, faithful wife and mother, and church member. Amanda is a woman of vision who is determined to be a generation challenger, and she travels the world delivering her message to many people.

With an insightful revelation of God's unlimited power to build His Kingdom, she dares to ask, *"Can a Nation Be Changed in a Day?"* Amanda uses both historical data and the Word of God to clarify and prove this possibility. This powerfully anointed book challenges readers, yet does so without leaving them in a guilty frame of mind. Amanda believes that each of us—by leaving the past behind, with all of its entanglements and traditions—is capable of experiencing the transformation of cities and nations.

You will discover fresh revelation of the Word as Amanda opens up stories of the real problems of Adam and Eve in the garden, the Prodigal Son, Peter's walk on the water, and other relevant Scriptures, all of which support her theme. Reformation begins with the individual, who can then influence society in general.

Can a Nation Be Changed in a Day? is not just another book about the need for revival. This book challenges and excites believers to set the course for generations to come. As we walk

in the light of His glory, which is our inheritance, the knowl-
edge of that glory fills the whole earth. That is global impact.
This book needed to be written now, and I'm so glad that
Amanda obeyed the Lord's direction to do so.

—*Iverna Tompkins*

Introduction

In 2002, the Lord spoke to me about writing books. In the ensuing months, this call was confirmed by a dream and a prophetic word, but also followed by days of dread! The thought of publishing my writing filled me with fear of failure and absolute terror! At school, I was not exactly known as the class scholar. I didn't do well in school—which is an understatement in itself. I always scored the lowest in the class, and when the students were separated into "turtles" and "rabbits," I took my place as the slowest of the turtles. After taking a career guidance test at 12 years old, the result was that my IQ most suited me for the occupation of janitor.

So when the Lord told me to write, I thought one of us had lost our minds! I asked Him if He had been stressed out lately, for surely He had the wrong lady. Then in 2003, I met two gentlemen—Don Nori and Pietro Evangelista—and that changed my life. They encouraged me, as no other colleagues had ever done before, and they believed in me. I wrote my first book in 2002, and it was released in January 2004. I almost needed to take Valium on its release date because thoughts of failure and humiliation plagued my every waking and sleeping moment.

Since I was eight years old, I have known the call of God was on my life. But at that age, and at that time, I thought, *What else could a woman be, but a nun?* There was one small problem with this: I grew up in a conservative Protestant home. My mission in life was to be a nun in the African Congo. (Isn't that where all nuns go?) Then at the age of 11, I saw *The Sound of Music* and fell madly in love with Christopher Plummer. Right then and there, I knew that my call in life was to go to Austria and marry Christopher Plummer—after I joined the convent!

At 15, I met my Lord and Savior and realized that I was no longer in love with Christopher, but with Jesus. The journey to where I am today was a long and tough one. Today, I look and see a wonderful husband, three gorgeous children, and a son-in-law. I have traveled to over 30 nations and have ministered in around 20 countries. When I finally ministered in Austria, I didn't find Christopher Plummer, but I did manage to imagine that I climbed one of the Alps. With God, all things are possible; He uses the foolish and confounds the wise!

As I sit at my computer completing the finishing touches to this, which is my second book, I am surrounded with news reports about the world's greatest tragedy in our history. On December 26, 2004, a huge tsunami hit with a destructive force; at early count, it devastated 12 nations and ended countless numbers of lives. The likes of a disaster this immense has never before been seen in our history. I have sat and pondered this event in prayer and have grieved for the families whose lives have been destroyed and will never again return to normality.

This book is based around the events of September 11, 2001, when the planet was rocked by a war of unseen attackers, called terrorists, who leveled the twin towers of the World Trade Center in New York City. But we could also see the parallels of today's events, as our planet has once again been struck with a disaster that affects every nation.

Our planet was created by the Word of God and is established and remains because of the Word of God. Yet, for centuries, man has attempted to institute kingdoms where man is a god, and, thus, remove the Creator of the universe from His place and position on the planet. We have seen men discover new lands and nations, in which we now reside, that had foundations established on His Word. But as soon as God's Kingdom is ruling, it seems that man wants to dethrone the One who created him and replace the Lord with a creation made from Creation itself. Again and again, man tries to rule and reign.

We find that man is full of empty promises. World War I brought global leaders together to make a covenant of peace, which led to the creation of the League of Nations. But this pact was fraught with problems—mainly man's frailty. World War II caused the dream of peace to shatter. The end of that conflict brought another somewhat problematic commitment to peace, which led to the birth of the United Nations. Yet, even this governing body could not eliminate the enemy within. Again, nations are plagued by "religious wars," as controlling rulers build kingdoms that allow foreign gods to invade our countries. It's all in an attempt to steal our peace, safety, and godly foundations and pollute the next generation.

Our planet has been in the midst of a severe trial, but has it propelled us back to our foundational roots? Whether that crucible has been wars, earthquakes, or tsunamis, the result should be to draw us closer to Him, not push us away. In Matthew 24 and 25, Jesus talks about the Kingdom and warns us that we will hear of wars, famines, and earthquakes. Who would have believed what would occur in the world 2,000 years later? We have terrorism in our backyard, which became a war on citizens; and a 9.0-rated earthquake ensued, when an 8.0 Richter scale quake is equivalent to detonating 6 million tons of dynamite!

In Matthew 13:11 (NAS), Jesus said, *"To you it has been granted to know the mysteries of the kingdom of heaven...."* Many of these mysteries are revealed in Isaiah 61, where Jesus gives us the key to unlocking the door to His Kingdom. Sadly, this Scripture has been interpreted in an evangelistic fashion; in so doing, what gets overlooked is that the apostolic Church is emerging with secrets of the Kingdom within her grasp.

In this book, I have attempted to unlock the mysteries within this passage of Scripture and allow us to see what Jesus meant when He read from this passage after returning from His wilderness experience. As I started to study this one Scripture, it seemed to contain unending mysteries that are eternal, just like the Word itself. I embarked upon a passionate search for the King and His Kingdom; it became a discovery of reformation that finished with the greatest journey of destiny I have ever been privileged to travel. The problem is: After writing it all down I realized that it would be a very long book. So, after discussions with my publisher, we decided to divide it into two volumes.

This is the first volume, and the journey begins with the discovery of His Kingdom and the pursuit of passion and understanding. I pray that this book will bring to you the door of your potential and destiny. May it birth within you an excitement for the future, and for what was and what can be. May you be left with an insatiable hunger for "His Kingdom to come in our nation and our lives!"

Chapter 1

A City Under Attack

The sun's gentle rays broke through the darkness and brought serenity and the promise of a beautiful day. Flawless skies offered 70 degrees as the mild heat carried a peaceful warmth and glow. A soft breeze tenderly rustled among the leaves on trees, which were slowly turning golden brown—colors that attested to a change of season. All of this presented the city with the beginnings of a pleasant, almost perfect autumn day—one that a bustling city would soon embrace.

In "the city that never sleeps," the sun's early rays seemed to transport it into a moderate, busy roar that would increase as the day went on. The night before was now a distant memory as the city's routine seemed to pave its own way. Faceless, nameless people began habitually moving forward at a hectic pace and, as all the activity increased, "the city that never sleeps" was again living up to its name.

As the sun's rays shone through September skies, men and women hurried into office blocks, joggers scurried onto subways, and computers on floors of every building were booted up. In an instant, those who kept the financial and cultural hub of the nation alive replaced those who lived in the city's night places.

A similar exchange was occurring in cities all over the country. In airport towers, casual good-byes and small talk could be heard as air traffic controllers finished their shifts and exchanged polite conversation with those on the next watch. Wafting through the air was the aroma of freshly brewed coffee, as the next shift of controllers concentrated on the flights at hand—they did not yet comprehend the magnitude of the day that lay ahead. Not one of these people realized that in only a few hours' time, a history-making event would occur, many lives would be shattered and forever changed, and terror would soon rule the skies.

At 7:45 a.m., at Boston's Logan International Airport, a flight attendant called a flight in a droning voice that attested to her having called this flight hundreds of times before. As the sleepy passengers were welcomed aboard an American Airlines Boeing 767—with the same, stale smile that had greeted thousands of faceless passengers previously—they saw no sign indicating that this flight was different from any others that had previously flown this route.

Flight attendants secured the cabin as the aircraft taxied out onto the runway. Passengers settled into their seats, reading newspapers, catching up on the news, hoping to relax with a cup of coffee before beginning a hectic day. After takeoff, the crew of Flight 11 concentrated on its 81 passengers. Following its flight plan, the aircraft headed west and soared over the Adirondack Mountains, bound for its destination of Los Angeles.

To air traffic control, this American Airlines flight seemed no different than any other flight on any other day. But it was terrifyingly different, and this flight would remain in the minds and heart of a nation for generations to come! This apparently ordinary flight to Los Angeles had passengers on board who were anything but ordinary, and who would unleash a terror never before experienced by any nation.

By 8:15 a.m., concerned air traffic controllers made a note to supervisors that Flight 11 had ignored the air traffic controller who granted permission for its climb to 31,000 feet. Concern soon turned to fear, as tension rose in the control tower. Flight 11 had turned off its transponder—the flight instrument that allows radar to pinpoint its precise location in the air. It was now apparent that the plane had a grave problem. The heartbeat of every air traffic controller increased with the adrenaline of each anxious moment.

Radar showed that Flight 11 had changed course and was now headed for New York City! It was now clear that a hijacking had taken place in American airspace. Air traffic control notified NORAD (North American Air Defense Command) that Flight 11, bound for Los Angeles, had been hijacked.

It was now 8:40 a.m., when suddenly, a phone rang and broke the mounting tension. Madeline Sweeney, a flight attendant onboard Flight 11, was calling Michael Woodward at American Airlines to report that a hijacking was in progress and that passengers had been wounded.

Disbelief and fear grabbed the hearts and minds of the air traffic controllers as they listened on speakerphone to the voice of Madeline Sweeney. In a wavering voice filled with emotion, she gave the seat number of several of the hijackers. The plane was now headed for New York City and was flying dangerously low, but still no one had any idea of the nightmare that lay ahead.

The clock was ticking by, and what actually only took minutes to transpire seemed like hours in that tower. People sweated profusely as they watched and listened helplessly to the events happening before them. The President had been notified, and all cities were now on high alert. Tears filled the eyes of those listening as Madeline quietly but emotionally explained what was happening aboard Flight 11. Then her final words came: "I see water and a building," and then she screamed into the phone, "Oh my God...!" Seconds later, all that was heard was a crash that sickened the very bones of everyone listening. The silence in the room was deafening, and the only movement was a silent teardrop as it finally splashed onto a controller's desk in what seemed like slow motion.

Meanwhile, walking hurriedly along a New York City street, a child held his father's hand and tugged at the large palm encompassing his. He pulled hard, which caused his father to come out of his reverie and re-enter the reality of his surroundings. As he peered into the morning skies, the child cried out, "Look, Daddy, they're doing it on purpose!" With an almost vice-like grip, the father instinctively seized the boy's hand, as he looked in disbelief at what was being played out in the sky above him! He immediately ran with his boy to safety and was unable to comprehend the horror of what had just taken place!

The first plane hit the World Trade Center's north tower at 8:46 a.m., ripping through the building's steel casing and setting its top floors ablaze. Onlookers thought it must have been a sonic boom, a construction site accident, or perhaps a freak lightning bolt on a lovely autumn day; at worst, it was a horrific airline accident—a plane lost altitude and was out of control, or a pilot tried to ditch a plane in the river and missed. But as the gruesome rains began falling—shards of glass, bits of plane, a tire, office furniture, a hand, a leg, and then entire bodies—people in the streets all stopped, looked, and then fell silent. As smoke rose and ash rained down from the sky, volumes of papers from the previous day's unfinished business now floated toward earth.

At 8:46 a.m., a nervous pilot and hijackers who had turned a huge jet into a missile had accomplished their task with American Airlines Flight 11. The city was now transformed into a virtual war zone. A fireball had engulfed the north tower of the World Trade Center. People were screaming and sobbing as terrified passersby ran for safety, amidst a scene of mayhem and ongoing disbelief. What had happened? Why did a passenger jet fly into the building? Was it an accident? No one realized the enormity of the event that had just occurred. What would follow would be a difficult task—for a nation to heal and reform itself in a struggle to find answers and justice for its people.

Sirens drowned out the noise of the passersby. Police struggled to bring control to this war zone. Fire engines, ambulances, and available policemen from every borough were called into the horrific scene. Almost instantly, a distant wail of sirens came from all directions on lower Manhattan. Louis Garcia was among the first medics on the scene. He reports, "There were people running over to us burned from head to toe. Their hair was burned off. There were compound fractures, arms and legs sticking out of the skin. One guy had no hair left on his head." He cried emotionally. Of the six patients in his first ambulance run, two died on the way to St. Vincent's Hospital.

Surely, this was an end to the chaos witnessed on the ground by disbelieving commuters and rescue workers! But the greater terror ahead could never have been predicted by those living in a nation founded on justice, peace, equality, and democracy. This nation prided itself on security and safety for each and every citizen. Yes, it did have enemies within, and major cities with crime rates far too high, but every citizen in every city believed their nation to be a fortress that would keep out every external national enemy!

However, Flight 11 was not the only airplane the terrorists would commandeer that day. At 7:58 a.m., United Airlines Flight 175—a Boeing 767 bound for Los Angeles—took off from Boston's Logan International Airport. (Three minutes after Flight 175 left Boston, United Airlines Flight 93, which was bound for San Francisco, was scheduled to leave Newark.) The nine-person crew and 56 passengers were oblivious to the horror being played out in the airspace above New York City. Cabin crewmembers focusing on their passengers' comfort were unaware of the ensuing danger. Again, terror had hit the skies and the path of Flight 175 was about to change.

At a different airport, at precisely 8:14 a.m., Flight 77 taxied out onto the runway of Dulles International Airport near Washington, D.C., and awaited clearance from air traffic control to take off. With 64 people aboard—who were totally oblivious to the drama occurring miles away in another state—the captain initiated liftoff and the plane climbed into beautiful, clear skies.

When town planners and architects designed Washington, D.C., to be the nation's capital, they did so with a deliberate intention that the city would intimidate the leaders of every nation to be entertained in this remarkable city. Now the city that was erected to humble great men was itself to be humbled by an unknown force!

Another hijacking was in progress at 8:45 a.m., at the same time that air traffic controllers were listening to Madeline Sweeney's final words before Flight 11 crashed into the World Trade Center. Again, controllers had to notify authorities that another flight had been taken over by terrorists and was also being re-routed to New York. At 9:01 a.m.—just 15 minutes after Flight 11 crashed into the north tower of the World Trade Center—Flight 175 was on a collision course with the other remaining tower.

Onlookers and rescue workers watched in horror and panic, many of them sick-to-the-stomach with what was taking place before their very eyes. Then, at 9:03 a.m., the second plane repeated the first drama and the blinding coda of smoke and debris crumbled atop the rescue workers trying to rescue survivors from the first trauma. As a nation watched speechless, the continuous sound of sirens seemed like an awful chorus that wailed on and on, letting them know that the horror was not over yet.

With no time for a rescue or to call people into a place of safety, everyone's worst nightmare was becoming a reality. The splitting sound of metal was heard in the already tense and noisy street. Balls of fire hurtled for miles around the city as the second plane, carrying 65 innocent lives, plunged into its fiery grave. The time was 9:03 a.m., and the city that never sleeps was thrust into a state of shock and grief never before felt during peacetime.

Minutes before, at 9:00 a.m., air traffic control had become aware of another fatal situation about to occur. Flight 77 had changed course and was heading straight for Washington, D.C. Just 37 minutes after that initial warning of danger, Flight 77 crashes into the Pentagon. To a nation's horror and disbelief, the unthinkable was happening before its very eyes. Shaken news reporters covering the story were unable to talk as sobs choked their throats. In one hour, they watched a wave of terror bring a city to its knees.

President George W. Bush had been notified of what had transpired in less than an hour in two of the nation's major cities, and was fully aware of the attack on his nation and its people. With security now on high alert and the White House and Pentagon evacuated, President Bush declared Washington, D.C., to be in a state of emergency at 1:27 p.m. that same afternoon. To bring a halt to these prevailing, perilous attacks, President Bush gives the directive to launch Air Force fighter jets into the airspace of Washington, D.C.

The nation looked to be at war. Certainly, the grief overwhelming the survivors and rescuers was as traumatic as that caused by any war. But this war was no ordinary war. An enemy that fully exposed itself was not waging this war on the United States. This evil force did not play by rules of engagement and fight on the fields of military men. This war was insidious; unknown men and women racked terror on an innocent, unprepared nation not trained for a war of terrorism. This hidden war incited fear and dread in the heart of a nation and its society!

Most Americans were reeling in horror as they watched TV reports showing live videos of the office towers of New York City being brought to rubble. Unbeknownst to them, another drama, initiated in another city, was still in progress. At Newark Airport in New Jersey, United Airlines Flight 93, with 44 passengers on board, took off headed for San Francisco. Originally scheduled to depart at 8:00 a.m., the flight was delayed and didn't actually take off until 8:47 a.m. While in the air, the news strikes the flight's passengers that three other planes have been hijacked that morning, and two have crashed into the World Trade Center and one into the Pentagon.

By 9:45 a.m., it was clear that Flight 93 was no longer being controlled by the United Airlines crew, but instead by terrorist hijackers. The passengers aboard Flight 93 knew that their path was doomed and headed for a collision course of destruction. With this in mind, some passengers realized that their fate was destined to be one of death. So, they decided to do everything within their power to halt at least one course of destruction on that fateful day. Some heroic men bravely confronted the armed terrorists. In the ensuing struggle to avert the subsequent hijacking, Flight 93 crashed in an empty field in Pennsylvania at 10:03 a.m. The courage of a few passengers, determined to prevent the terrorists' mission from being accomplished, saved many lives.

By 1:00 p.m. on the East Coast, the nation had come to a standstill. All passenger airliners were halted and all those with flight plans to the United States were diverted to other nations. A city stood in disbelief, and a horrified nation could not comprehend what had just transpired on that autumn morning. As New York Mayor Rudy Giuliani rushed out of his downtown office to look at the war zone, terror gripped his heart and confirmed the fear and revulsion that his eyes tried to comprehend. What he saw were immeasurable acres of devastation. Firefighter uniforms blended in with civilian clothes and both intermingled with the rubble, with only the uniforms' reflective bands casting any recognizable difference.

Screams of terror, shrills of sirens, policemen yelling orders! Firemen and paramedics briefed each other as they tried to restore order in a city wracked with panic and fear. Mayor Rudy Giuliani's eyes were wet with unshed tears as he saw a society under assault from an unknown enemy, as he said, "We don't know yet how many people have died, but once we know, it will be more than we can bear."

THE CITY WAS NEW YORK.

THE NATION WAS THE
UNITED STATES OF AMERICA.

THE DATE STAMPED INDELIBLY
IN THE HEARTS AND MINDS
OF EVERY CITIZEN WAS:

SEPTEMBER 11th 2001

Chapter 2

Code Red: A Day of Terror

If you want to humble an empire, it is reasonable to presume that you would mutilate its churches and cathedrals. These are the nation's symbols of faith. When they fold and burn, the authority and core beliefs that the nation is built on are ravished, and that causes its people to feel vulnerable. The twin towers of the World Trade Center, fixed at the foot of Manhattan Island with the Statue of Liberty as its guard, were acknowledged as the refuge of money and power that defined America. The Pentagon is a colossal concrete structure on the banks of the Potomac, a fortress that guards the strategies of the nation's military. Its enemies assumed that America's faith was built on a foundation of unadulterated materialism of "what they can buy and build," but they were wrong—that has never been America's true God.

America's foundation can be seen in the aphorism "In God We Trust." On that fateful day, truer words never meant more to a society than those words declared by America's forefathers when founding U.S. independence. September 11th, 2001, was the bloodiest day on American soil since the Civil War. It was a modern tragedy played out in real time and in fast forward—not with soldiers, but with secretaries, security guards, lawyers, bankers, cleaners, moms, and dads. That day marked the birth of modern-day terrorism in the West.

That day of war was a strange time because suddenly a nation stood motionless in disbelief. No one could move; it was as if eternity had suddenly frozen and time no longer existed. Perhaps that was the intent, so the world had no choice but to watch as a nation stood paralyzed. Every nation on the planet was aware of what horror had struck the impenetrable superpower on that day. News reporters interrupted scheduled programs and declared that the unthinkable was being played out before the world's eyes! Drums in the deepest part of Africa were beating the change in the course of history. Radio stations broke into programs on every continent and spoke forth the news that "America is at war with terrorists." No one on the planet old enough to feel the weight of the magnitude of what had happened can forget where he or she was the moment they heard the words!

Every city recorded its targets. Residents looked at their skylines and wondered if they would be the same when they awoke from this living nightmare. Stock exchanges all over the world held their breath. Could this cause a crash as the one that preceded the Great Depression? The Sears Tower in Chicago was evacuated, as were all colleges and museums. Terrified parents were seizing their children from classes in schools all over America, taking them home to what used to be a safe haven. Disney World shut down, and Major League Baseball canceled its games. Three Mile Island (in Pennsylvania) and other nuclear power plants went to top security status—Code Red. The Hoover Dam and the Mall of America shut down. Independence Hall in Philadelphia, and Mount Rushmore in South Dakota were evacuated and closed.

The United States prepared to go into lockdown mode as the government raised the nation's terror alert to *Code Red*, which is the highest threat level for terrorism. *Code Red means there is a severe risk of terrorist attack, or that an attack is imminent or may already be under way*. It was as if someone had taken a gigantic paintbrush and painted a bull's-eye around every place that Americans gather—every revered icon and every service that the nation depended on—and swore to take them out, shut them down or, even worse, to destroy them.

On an ordinary day, heroism is honored and valued because it is exceptional and unusual. On September 11, America esteemed heroism because it was necessary and it was everywhere. Firefighters kept climbing the stairs of the tallest buildings in New York—even though its steel groaned and cracks widened in the walls—just to rescue the people trapped. Valor was even being played out in the streets, as escaping victims pulled the wounded to safety. At every hospital, the lines to give blood circled round the block. Medical supply companies were sending supplies without being asked. One worker threw on a New York Fire Department jacket just so he could go in and save people. All across the nation, people sought for some way to help. What the enemy sought to destroy and bring division into only assisted in drawing a nation into unity.

It's difficult to comprehend not only how some people were extricated from the fiery heap, but how some actually survived. Some victims' families were only able to collect a splinter of bone to place in a coffin, as they laid a loved one to rest. They then had the rest of their lives to attempt to come to terms with their grief and rage and to find an answer to an unanswerable question!

By 10:28 a.m. on September 11, almost everyone who had not escaped the twin towers had perished. On the 64th floor of the north tower, some should have left earlier, but they delayed due to fear and uncertainty of what was happening and of where to seek safety. After booting up a computer, a worker carrying breakfast walked a few steps and stopped to chat with a friend at a nearby desk. While whispering the latest office gossip, the floor suddenly shook and they heard a piercing roar; they thought that it was a sonic boom! As the building gave an almighty shake, it knocked one man out of his chair and onto the floor.

Unaware that American Airlines Flight 11 had just penetrated the building upstairs—in a diagonal fashion on floors 94 to 98—one worker cried out, "What the hell?" Not yet scared but curious, another woman left her breakfast and investigated at the window. Petrified and confused, she sees a snowstorm of papers in the air;

she then stood in dread and confusion, frozen to the spot. Soon after, high-pitched voices were screaming that a plane had hit the building. Unable to comprehend what had transpired—and hearing her heart pound in her chest because of adrenaline pumping through her veins—she heard a voice yelling, "We have to leave. Get your stuff now, and let's get out of here."

As employees tried to escape by scuttling down stairway B, the stairwell burst beneath them, and they landed atop an unstable pile of debris. Unexpectedly, the entire building collapsed. Some people were buried alive; others mortally wounded by plunging chunks of stone and metal; others were compressed in mini-collapses in the later hours of September 11; and some were burned in voracious fires. The terror seemed never-ending, like a nightmare that refused to come to a close.

Unquestionably, the city had now entered a phase of confusion and grief, which would eventually settle into indignation and fury experienced by every man, woman, and child in the country. Fear and terror played out that morning like a musical masterpiece by an elite orchestra—it had many diverse instruments (all in perfect tune) that played flawlessly in complete unison, so as to achieve its desired effect. Its crescendo was grief that brought mourning, sorrow, cries of horror, and terror. As a world watched, thunderstruck, the sirens cried out in time to the people's mourning—minute after minute, hour after hour—and caused a nation to realize that its impenetrable fortress had been penetrated by an unseen, internal power.

That day showed the world that we are all acutely susceptible to a destructive force. In some ways, its potency was more dangerous, and certainly more insidious, than any tyrannical power that the world has previously attacked and defeated. This enemy refused to fight with honor; it concealed and withdrew itself, and even vanished into the mayhem, only to re-emerge whenever its purposes were served.

This enemy cannot be assaulted as have other external enemies of the past because it's more like a virus than a host; it infects and captures a nation and then progresses to suck the life out of another. How does a nation resist such an unseen enemy? How does an individual prevent a cancer from eating away at the very molecular formulation of oneself as a human being? How does a nation resist an enemy that wants to devour its core confidence, worth, and status as an integral part of the globe?

The focus of terrorists in society had suddenly evolved. No longer were terrorists targeting diplomatic heads, military officials, and politicians, but they had shifted to targeting the general public. September 11 showed that for the first time in history, America—land of the free, home of the brave to millions—was actually vulnerable and defenseless to a lethal foreign foe called *terrorism*. In 12 hours, the dreams, ideals, thoughts, hopes, and expectations of countless lives were left in immeasurable fragments on a footpath. Tired, faceless heroes were left to pick up the pieces of what was once an existence!

This adversary's mind-set was simple: If we take out the head, then the hands won't work! By attacking America, the enemy thought they would stop her allies from fighting back. That presumption was to prove erroneous; for when you attack the head of a Christian community, the hands do fight back! The United States, Australia, and their allies may not agree on all the same philosophies, but they do connect in unity of purpose, values, and beliefs. The enemy was unaware that Psalm 133:1-3 would be the allies' strength: *"Behold how good and how pleasant it is for brethren to dwell together in unity...for there the Lord commanded a blessing—Life forevermore."* Even in 2004, as both American and Australian voters went to the polls, its peoples chose unity and men of God over unrighteous policies.

But it was not long before the enemy arose on the shores of the West, and another internal war against normal people shook the world. When the Sari Club, a nightclub in Bali, was bombed on October 12, 2002, Westerners were the targets. After a peaceful, sleepy nation known for its tourist resorts reeled from the shock, it realized that 202 people had been killed, and

88 of them were Australians. Now Australia had become a target of an unseen enemy! Bali bombers later admitted that Australians were deliberately targeted, as they were allies of the United States.

The enemy seems to have overlooked one commonality about Australia and the United States; both these nations are undergirded by something stronger than money, consumerism, or even patriotism: a strong foundation that God is their protector, and the nation stands in faith in Him. The very words declared over both nations on the day of their foundation represents that belief. Job 22:28 says, *"You will also declare a thing, and it will be established for you; so light will shine on your ways."* In these two nations, the day their constitution was written and delivered was the day when their foundation on Almighty God was established.

THE AMERICAN CONSTITUTION

The Preamble

"We the people of the United States, in order to form a more perfect union, establish justice, ensure domestic tranquillity, provide for the common defense, promote the general welfare, and secure the blessings of liberty to ourselves and our posterity, do ordain and establish this Constitution for the United States of America."

THE CONSTITUTION OF AUSTRALIA

The Preamble

"Whereas the people of New South Wales, Victoria, South Australia, Queensland, and Tasmania humbly relying on the blessing of Almighty God, have agreed to unite in one indissoluble Federal Commonwealth under the Crown of the United Kingdom of Great Britain and Ireland, and under the Constitution hereby established."

When these constitutions were formulated, they represented the heartbeat and raw belief of the nation. It declared to every other nation or empire what principles and beliefs these new colonies trusted to be true about their newfound nation! Never before in the history of peacetime was this ideology and truth to be tested, as it was on the days of these terrorist attacks. Not only were prime ministers, presidents, senators, and congressmen put to the test, but also every individual who called themselves an Australian or an American—whether black, white, Asian, or Indian. On this day, the allegiance to their flags was tested, the words to their anthems tried, and their strength as human beings stretched to limits none could have conceived to be possible.

Some have expressed these horrific events as a *crucible* to these nations. If not for the nation, then it was undoubtedly a crucible for the survivors. For them, it epitomized the meaning of the word *crucible*, which is a severe trial, in which different elements interact to produce something new. The dilemma facing the future of this generation would not only be in who emerged from the smoldering crucible, but in the actual change now produced on the entire society. This is what would finally matter in the end. Two nations arose from the rubble as a horror-struck world watched in total disbelief; suddenly, they realized that the impossible had not only become plausible, but also achievable.

NATIONS HAD BEEN REFORMED *BY EVIL*

IN ONE SINGLE DAY!

CODE RED

Chapter 3

How Reformation Affects Society

Martin Luther (1483-1546) was positioned in church and secular history as an exceptional influence. By pure willpower, passion, and zeal, this individual broke new frontiers to change the face of the world fundamentally through religion, and, therefore, transform the marketplace. Luther (and the reformation he single-handedly brought into Europe) never truly wanted to symbolize a break with the past. Rather, it was to be an explosion in time to become a turning point in God's eternal plan. Dreams, ideas, and developments that had been smoldering in Europe for several centuries suddenly approached a point of combustion.

Luther's efforts and new thoughts permanently changed the earth and pressed it toward a place in the modern era from which it would never return. Yet, Luther was not a person you would take home to meet your mother, or spend a leisurely afternoon with. He was volatile, irritable, egomaniacal, and contrary.

In some ways, he had developed his faith externally, but his internal makeup had not been transformed by his beliefs. On the other hand, his single-mindedness, colossal self-confidence, and raucous belief of his own arguments are what permitted him to stand against opponents. He could set his face like flint in the face of death by fire, which was the standard punishment for heretics in his era.

His walk with God, and total belief in the truth of His Word, is what started a movement that finally led the Church out of darkness. Even during the Dark Ages, God had a remnant who would hear and obey Him, even in the face of death. No matter how dark a nation gets, remember that God always has a person who will break through that society and impact a nation to transform a generation.

Luther's strident beliefs caused him to nail the 95 Theses on the door of Wittenberg Castle Church, which was considered an outrage by the Pope, the Cardinal, and the Catholic Church. As he walked down that road with the Theses in hand, Luther could only have been driven by his passionate pursuit for Christ and for change, as he strode past enemies of his beloved Christ. Indeed, the outcome was not completely as Luther would have desired. His passion was to bring truth back into society and the religious world, but that same truth would also cause an irreparable split between religious factions and churches.

Nailing those papers to the church door did not immediately change the spiritually dark and decaying condition of the Church. Reformation creates momentum in society, causing it to go forward in an ongoing reformation. *"Ecclesia reformanda, semper reformata"* means "the reformed church is always being reformed." That Latin phrase was the Reformation's motto, and it still applies to the Church today.

REFORMATION—THE CATALYST FOR TECHNOLOGICAL BREAKTHROUGHS

Technological reform was inevitable as word spread throughout Germany of new reforms coming to the Church. These reforms soon became a catalyst for technology to develop. Luther's 95 Theses, and his other works, were distributed throughout Germany quickly. For the first time, the printing press was used to spread reformatory or revolutionary ideas; the commotion that started in the Church was now of interest to all sectors of society. Previously, the printing press had only been used for academic texts.

In 1450, Johannes Gutenberg, revolutionized printing. He did not invent the printing press, as it is often understood; rather, he invented a new printing process that made it possible to print works quickly and cost-efficiently through the usage of individual metal letters. Suddenly, the Reformation and its advances impacted the minds and hearts of every strata of society—from theologians to the higher class. The new process of printing now made these works accessible and readily available to all levels of society.

The Reformation is the force that created the inevitable outcome of discoveries in science and literature. As mass printing became accessible, classical pieces of literature in original languages became circulated, which sparked intellectual debate and re-evaluation of conservative, conventional thoughts. The wide impact of Luther's translation of the Bible into German, and the emergence in England of a King James Version of the Bible is due, in part, to the effect of Reformation on societal developments. Breakthroughs in technology and science and the discovery of new lands began to happen faster than humanity itself could cope with. Princes in Germany were excited, as they saw this theological revolution as an economic/political opportunity to create wealth.

REFORMATION LED TO NEW FRONTIERS OPENING UP

America

Suddenly, the world was going through an enormous upheaval of change and transition. Religion and technology seemed to be on a collision course—one that would bring all of civilization into a new, modern era that forever forsook past beliefs. Reformation had transformed an entire society. No matter how the politicians, kings, princes, or theologians of the day struggled to keep a grip on the past, it was now impossible; the world was in *the middle of a crucible of change, bringing with it a new epoch or era in civilization.*

During this time, a newfound frontier called America was also in the process of change. Reformation had left its handprint on this new land as well. America was unique in its beginnings; it was founded and developed by a people with a strong Reformation spirit. The Scottish Presbyterians, under the leadership and teachings of John Knox, laid a foundation of democracy in the early Americas and its people.

Reformation had already touched America in the early 1600s, during the height of the Protestant-Catholic wars and throughout the Reformation that encompassed Europe. Technology and science were advancing dramatically, and the abounding knowledge led to great developments in both fields. This dramatic change brought an urgency to declare the core beliefs and democracy that the new frontier immersed itself in, as settling pioneers developed daily boundaries.

An assembly of leaders gathered in Philadelphia (in 1776) to assert the right of every American to reject tyranny and exercise a right for democracy. King George III of Britain could see that he was losing his grip on the subjects in the colony. So, he enlarged his increasing resolve to position himself. As a means of shattering their spirit, he increased a tyrannical reign not only on the colonies, but on the people living in them.

These new leaders needed to fight to preserve that which had already been intensely embedded in the American persona from the Reformation of its founders. In 1776, the start of a *revolution* (meaning "dramatic change") broke out. The American colonies had a determination to maintain its rights, customs, and character as a separate community, which was divided from Europe by thousands of miles and also by religious, cultural, and political development.

King George III had not taken into account that he was coming up against a profound sense of religious, cultural, and political values. That drive for ideology caused these American colonists to rise up in indignation at the very idea that tyranny would challenge their foundational nucleus to become an ultimate judge, leader, and ruler of their fate. That honor belonged to God alone.

These American colonists were Calvinist Protestants. A people who had made a "covenant" or vow of their lives to God, they promised to follow His guidance in building their new "promised land" of America. They referred to their nation as a "City on a Hill," which was erected to give pure, unadulterated Christian light to the rest of the world.

They were willing to accept huge sacrifices, and the pioneers who endeavored to settle in America understood that risk. But they did so in order to follow through faithfully on this covenant to God. Indeed, when around half of the members who came to the Plymouth colony died during their first winter in America (1620-21), not one single survivor abandoned the project. The Mayflower returned to England the next summer. Obviously, they were there for the long haul—even if it cost their lives.

Then, suddenly and without warning, a strange phenomenon swept through the colonies. A religious revival of first-century Pentecostals was catching up with America. Going from north to south, it hit an emotional peak in the early 1740s. Nothing like this had ever been experienced before in anyone's memory, even in historical recollection. No one was expecting it, much less planning or engineering it. It just rose up and seized America.

This "Great Awakening" brought out hundreds of thousands of common people who were looking for spiritual and emotional respite from the harshness of pioneering a new land. They came from miles around—by horse, in wagons, and on foot—and stood for hours, while entranced by messages of judgment and hope carried by itinerant preachers. At first, local churches entertained these "revivals." But soon, the throng of people infinitely surpassed the churches' capability to house those in attendance. Thousands gathered in open fields; even in Philadelphia, an open-air meeting drew 20,000 people at one gathering alone.

The hard, treacherous times caused by breaking into new frontiers was the apparent crucible needed for the nation to come into sociological, technological change, and to fashion a godly structure in its foundation. The people's passion was to create a new nation built on core beliefs: freedom, domestic peace, secure blessings of liberty and truth, and justice for themselves and generations to come.

In one day, men and women birthed America with a Reformation spirit. They were willing to undergo any hardships from a foreseeable threat of outside forces. The reason? To preserve the spirit that America had been conceived by. As Christians, we need to reflect on our foundations and recognize the hand of God on our nations. America was being birthed from the seed of Reformation, and a great awakening was taking place. Meanwhile, on the other side of the world, another unknown frontier was being discovered and stamped with a Reformation spirit.

Australia

[Most of the information in this section is taken directly from "Australia's Christian Heritage" by Graham McLennan at: http://www.outbackpatrol.com.au/heritage.htm.]

Many Australians look to their nation's past as a penal colony—which produced a fear of authority, a spirit of rebellion, and feelings of inferiority and isolation. But there is another history. That legacy is of our Christian forefathers, whose faith and contribution to the Kingdom of God creates a positive affirmation of a nation with a providential destiny.

A Portuguese Catholic explorer, Ferdinand Magellan, is the one who opened up the South Seas to the Europeans. Magellan's main purpose was to convert unknown, barbaric nations to Christ. His faith sustained him through terrible deprivations, while he searched for and found a strait into the Pacific. Pedro Fernandez de Quiros, another Portuguese Catholic, was also seeking to convert inhabitants of the South Seas to Christianity. Quiros believed that he had finally discovered a great expanse of land, where he declared, *"La Terra Australia del Espiritu Santo,"* or "Southland of the Holy Spirit." He dedicated the land to the Holy Spirit and described it as the region of the south, as far as the pole.

The first Christian minister came with the first fleet. Richard Johnson (who was highly recommended by Evangelical churchmen John Newton and William Wilberforce) took many Bibles, Books of Common Prayer, Psalters, and numerous booklets against common sins. On Sunday, February 3, 1788, Johnson conducted the first Christian service on Australian soil, using Psalm 116:12: "What shall I render to the Lord for all His benefits toward me?"

For many years, South Australia's capital was known as the Holy City, but today it is known as the City of Churches. In its formative years, the city of Adelaide couldn't seat all the parishioners in its churches. During Adelaide's first eight years, there were more preachers and places of worship than in the first decade in the New England area of the United States. From the time of South Australia's settlement (1836 to 1915), more children attended Sunday school than attended secular schools.

England's "Evangelical Awakening" also had its effect on Australia. Through reading *Captain Cooks Voyages*, people such as William Carey became awakened to the need for evangelizing heathen lands. It was the first time that many English became aware of lands within the Pacific Ocean and in regions of Asia. Commencing in 1784, the Baptists (and other non-conformists throughout the Midlands) began meeting for an hour on the first Monday of each month to pray for revival. Soon, that revival force would spread the gospel to the globe's most distant parts.

This marked the beginning of the Christian faith's greatest period of expansion since apostolic times. Most of the Australian colony's early leadership came from the evangelical Christian community. Governors such as Hunter, Macquarie, and Brisbane, and a number of officials, such as Judge Advocates John Wylde and Ellis Bent and the editor of Australia's first newspaper, had strong commitment to Christian views, as did the schoolteachers.

Governor Macquarie was always trying to improve the colony's moral and religious well-being; he hoped that those in his care would become good Christians. He personally promoted the British and Foreign Bible Society and the Sunday School Movement.

James Stephen, the permanent Under Secretary of the Colonial Office, believed that God was going to use Australia as a Christian nation; he was influential in choosing many Christian leaders for the colony. Among them was George Arthur, who shared with James Stephen the vision of Australia as being the Christian base in Southeast Asia and the Pacific to reach Chinese, Hindu, and Muslim nations to the north.

Another example of a strong Christian in Australian history is Captain Charles Sturt, a great Australian pioneer and heroic inland explorer. He was a man of considerable courage, faith, and prayer. Throughout the pages of his journals, Sturt shared his faith constantly, especially when writing to his wife. He used to pray continually for guidance and committed each day's journey to God.

Australians can rejoice in the contribution of our Christian forefathers and confidently step out in faith with an awareness of God's great intentions for our island continent. We must remind ourselves, and the generation that follows, *that if the past is misinterpreted, then so is the significance of the future.* Psalm 61:5 says, *"You have given me the heritage of those who fear Your name."* If our heritage is firmly grounded on Christianity and the sovereignty of Almighty God, then who can come against us and try to destroy us!

We must never forget an overwhelming truth: If evil can change a nation in a single day—as when America and Australia were hit by a wicked, terrorist foe threatening to steal core beliefs that national constitutions are based on—then "good" can and will have the same effect. Let us put it this way: If the devil can change a nation in a day by humiliating it and bringing it to its knees, then surely prophetic words of Isaiah can come to pass in a single day! *"Who has heard such a thing? Who has seen such things? Shall the earth be made to give birth in one day? Or shall a nation be born [reformed] at once?"* (Isa. 66:8) Or, in modern terminology, we could say: *"Can a Nation Be Changed in a Day?"*

As we have seen through history,

it is not only a plausible, but also a conceivable
FACT THAT

IF EVIL CAN CHANGE THE COURSE OF HISTORY
IN ONE DAY,

then God can also bring a reformation into our
NATIONS IN A SINGLE MOMENT OF TIME!

Therefore our only answer is:

"YES!"

Chapter 4

A Passionate Cause

If an enemy attack of such proportions could change the lives of so many, and alter a nation's history on one single day, then couldn't we as believers in Christ do the same? It is now a qualified fact that Muslim extremists often conceal themselves in groups, like Hezbollah, Mujahedin, and Al Qaeda. Such groups believe themselves to be defending the "kingdom of Islam." In the light of facts that arose from law enforcement agencies and governmental sources after September 11, one can assume that these groups consider their kingdom to be at war with the U.S. and its allies.

The roots of Hezbollah, Mujahedin, and Al Qaeda go back hundreds of years. Now their fundamental credence is to train a military force and organize a well-planned, efficient intelligence organization that constructs a cell-based functioning structure. The Mujahedin goes so far as to incorporate traditional, tribal customs in an array of horrific tortures to be inflicted upon enemies. Even advanced intelligence sources in progressive Western nations are finding it almost impossible to attain mastery over this revolution of evil. These extremists globalize themselves by insidiously integrating themselves into almost every Western nation and becoming part of that nation's social structure and culture. Soon, they recruit others from the culture in which they are now integrated as members to join their fundamental cause.

The only way of stopping this insidious virus of terrorism is through the strength of character of the attacked nations to overcome evil by pursuing fresh information (or revelation) that serves a practical, successful purpose. If this should happen with the nation's citizens, then we will be on the verge of a reformation. If only individual interests are advanced, and not those of nations, then we have touched revival, but definitely not reformation.

The mission of extremist groups and those of the Church are miles apart, but they do share some similarities. Although we definitely don't want to give unnecessary praise to these evildoers, what can we possibly learn from the little we do know of their mission?

The Church is the Army of the Lord, and our hands trained for battle. As opposed to extremist groups, the Church does not fight against flesh-and-blood, for our fight is with an unseen enemy in an unseen realm. We, the Church, are the Body of Christ—every cell, bone, and joint is knit closely to work together to provide one living, breathing whole. That is the Body of Christ, which is the fullness of the Godhead! The Body of Christ does not need an intelligence agency, like the extremist groups do, for we have the mind of Christ, who is All in All.

The commission of these extremist groups is to integrate their members into other cultures and "evangelize" or "proselytize" every nation. The Bible tells the Church that although we are not of this world, we must live in it, subdue it, and have dominion over it; we are to be witnesses of His Kingdom in Jerusalem, Judea, Samaria, every continent, and to the ends of the earth!

Why then has the Church failed in its overall mission, but evil succeeded? These men and women of evil intent, all have one thing in common: They are *passionate* for their cause! They live and die for the cause they believe explicitly in. For most extremists, it is an honor to die for the cause. In World War II, Japanese kamikaze pilots considered it the greatest honor to be a martyr for Emperor and country. They would proudly wear their flag—the red symbol of the rising sun—tied on their forehead, which represented allegiance to Japan. Their weapon was not death itself, but the fear they inflicted on the enemy!

As the Church of the Lord Jesus Christ, it is time that we became as passionate for our cause as evildoers are in theirs! We have seen Christian extremists act in the name of the Lord, yet afterward, one would have to ask, "Which Lord were they acting in the name of?" Sadly, when some Christians gave their heart to the Lord, they also seemed to give up their brains as well. Would we be safe in saying that since Jesus left us with a brain to reflect on our actions that therefore He doesn't want it back? Passion is not stupidity, folly, or foolhardy behavior—it is a state of being and inner intensity that allows us to act appropriately, 100 percent for our cause, and to do so intelligently, wisely, and astutely!

"To whom also He showed Himself alive after His passion *by many infallible proofs, being seen of them forty days, and speaking of the things pertaining to the kingdom of God"* (Acts 1:3 KJV). Jesus Himself was passionate and focused on the Cross; so much so, that Calvary was called *His Passion.* His Cause became enveloped in passion!

We have looked at those in history, good and evil, who—through a total commitment and passion for a cause they believed in—have changed the course of history and a nation's destiny; by some means, these people succeeded in reforming the society and generation at hand. As another example, in the 1960s, four British lads (known as the Beatles) passionately believed in music. That passion changed a generation and altered the face of music. The Fab Four even named one of their albums *Revolution.*

Christians and churches have become hungry for revival. Although this is an excellent pursuit, history reveals that most revivals only last an average of five to seven years before burning out. These revivals are not passed down to the next generation, but are often centered around platform ministry. Soon after, they slowly perish and leave programs in their place with ministers running around as they try to bring the next "in" thing back to the church! Each year, thousands of dollars are made by well-meaning churches that sell revival packages to download a weekly "revival message." For a certain amount of money, you can host a "revivalist" at your church, and he will "bring" revival! But to see true reformation, we must go back not to Martin Luther's day, but to when the world's greatest revivalist breathed on the Church and created its birth!

Earlier, we established that it's feasible, plausible, and achievable to reform, change, and completely transform a nation in one day—because it has already been done before, by those who have used the power for evil. If we are to be a passionate people, then we must understand what passion is and how to focus it on our cause! Today, we see people passionate for cars and hobbies. But if they were put in a position of having to give their life for the subject at hand, it is doubtful that they would.

It's safe to say that a fan of Manchester United's soccer club would not be so enthusiastic if a knife was placed at his throat and he was asked to die for them! Many sports supporters hold up signs declaring how a certain player is "God!" If asked to sacrifice their life for that player, would they still believe him to be God? I don't think so. A secular example of passion—which is often confused with lust—is not the type of passion we are trying to explain. So what is the passion we are speaking of here, and how do we define it?

If passion drove Jesus to die for the cause of Heaven, then we can assume that passion is the dynamic that keeps the "cause" in a position of advancement. If Jesus showed Himself alive to His disciples *after His Passion*, then obviously that passion put Christ Jesus on the Cross, and also placed Him on the finish line of Resurrection and Ascension. Passion is not just a feeling, as feelings are not substance. Passion must be more than emotion, for both feelings and emotions can be in a state of instability and change. If passion was the cause of the Cross, then it is obvious that more than mere emotion moved Jesus to desire to die. But passion must have been a dynamic with potency, strength, and authority within it, and one that's intangible and indisputable.

Passion causes a zeal to burn in our hearts that affects our thinking patterns and, in turn, our behavior. *"For as he thinks in his heart, so is he"* (Prov. 23:7). A man's passion causes him to constantly meditate on what he is passionate about. Eventually, these thought patterns will cause him to behave differently.

"Because zeal for Your House has eaten me up..." (Ps. 69:9). A passion to build the Lord a place where He could dwell is what drove King David both day and night. Although unable to build a "house" for God, his son eventually built "the passion" that consumed and drove his father's thoughts. Passion, therefore, is generational and is substance that can be left as a heritage to the next generation. Passion burning within men and women's hearts will change the road they are walking today and allow them to rise up into a destiny of tomorrow!

"Did not our heart burn within us while He talked with us on the road...?" (Luke 24:32) Two men on a road of grief and sorrow were touched by passion, and then their hearts were consumed with a fire that burned deeply and eternally changed their "way." Passion will produce an intensity that not only changes our thought patterns, but will eventually mold our character.

> *And when He was twelve years old, they went up to Jerusalem...so it was that after three days they found Him in the temple, sitting in the midst of the teachers, both listening to them and asking them questions...And Jesus increased in wisdom and stature and in favor with God and men* (Luke 2:42,46,52).

Passion was the continual dynamic that pressed Jesus to do His Father's will, and it also built His character. Remember, although Jesus was 100 percent God, He was also 100 percent man! The dynamic of passion was why the adult Jesus looked at the same city where He learned and was secure in His Father's house, but now wept and lamented so passionately, "Oh Jerusalem, Jerusalem!"

The dynamic within passion is the essence that causes us to rise above our greatest limitations. A passionate person has no justification or excuses; he or she sees an obstacle as an opportunity for greatness, and not as problem that cannot be overcome. A passionate person realizes every problem has the seed of solution.

> *And when they had laid many stripes on them, they threw them [Paul and Silas] into prison, commanding the jailor to keep them securely...But at midnight Paul and Silas were praying and singing hymns to God, and the prisoners were listening to them (Acts 16:23,25).*

After being beaten for their *cause*, the dynamic of passion worked within both these men and they found focus amidst great limitations and calamity. With that driving force, they walked triumphantly through great suffering!

Joseph was another man who had passion to see a God-given dream come to pass. In a moment of exuberance, he told his brothers a dream of his future greatness. A jealous rage caused them to try to kill their young brother, and his dream along with it. Their mission was aborted, but not before Joseph was taken from the pit and made a prisoner in Potiphar's house. Through conditions that would have crushed most young men, Joseph passionately overcame every limitation as a prisoner. He eventually became one of the greatest men in Egypt and saw his vision come to pass. Passion kept his dream and destiny alive.

Passion must have tangible focus and purpose. If not, then it will become an emotion governed by feelings and will not work itself into a concrete substance. Esteemed pastor John Osteen once said, "Great it is to dream the dream when you stand in youth by the starry stream: But a greater thing is to fight life through and say at the end 'The dream is true!'" Dreaming passionately is not enough—that passion must outwork itself into a tangible dream! Passionate people are never lazy or lethargic; for a passionate person, time is of the essence, and every moment an opportunity. We must have intensity and passion, or we will never build into the life of the Church or the nation!

Dr. Jonathan David so aptly describes passion as this: "Time creates urgency, and urgency creates passion." What does this mean? Here is a simple example: A man and a woman, who are deeply in love, have only a few hours left together because one of them is about to die! Surely, the lack of time has created urgency to say to each other all that is in their hearts; their love is now exposed in raw emotion, and passion is created by urgency of the hour. The couple's fears come alive and expose the deepest emotions that have possibly been suppressed until now.

King David was a passionate man full of raw emotion. His psalms are an indication of what was in his heart. Psalm 17 reflects the essence of the man and his heart-cry for God alone. David had been constantly under the pursuits and threats of Saul; these betrayals and injustices caused him to become the man he was destined to be and to burn with a consuming passion for the Lord. *"Hear, a just cause, O Lord, attend to my cry; give ear to my prayer…"* (Ps. 17:1).

This is the exclamation of the desperate heart: no smoothly crafted words or eloquence here, but just raw emotion giving way to a heartfelt plea. David fears for his life and is smarting under the injustices and false accusations of Saul. Perplexed and finding refuge in the wilderness, he is crying out to God for vindication. The word translated here as "cry" is very powerful in the Hebrew—it refers to a "ringing cry." It is the cry of desperation that pierces Heaven with its intensity and urgency.

The Pilgrim's Progress author John Bunyan said, "When we pray, it is better to let our heart be without words, than for our words to be without heart." Or, could he have also said "passion"? Only a passionate person understands the urgency of the time he lives; only such a person can pierce the very courts of Heaven and strike a chord of emotion into the heart of the One sitting on the Throne. This cry will then cause a reverberation to sound, and not only around Heaven, but into the very nation itself!

David's fellowship—which flowed out of a profound relationship with God—caused the deepest desire in His heart to become a personal passion. Never before had God told anyone that His passion was that He sought a house. He had spoken to Moses to build a temple, but this was so man could draw closer to a Holy God. Now, God's desire was to have a place that He could not only inhabit, but also become the father of His House. This revelation had not been given to any man until Jesus came, and He spoke of God as now being Father of the house!

Passion produced intensity in relationship that allowed David to seize the desire of God's heart, and that, in turn, produced vision. When a relationship with Christ develops, He will then articulate the depths of His heart into our spirit. To find this intensity and develop it, we must increase our capacity for deeper communion with God.

Allowing my thoughts to dwell on passion in my soul will, in turn, create an intensity that causes my body to respond. This then creates excellence in what we are passionate about. Remember, whatever a man meditates on in his heart (meaning mind, as that is where we meditate), he then becomes that. Perhaps, we do not see an excellent spirit in the Body of Christ, due to lack of passion.

Passion can also be received through impartation from a passionate man or woman. The intensity of that person's spirit connects with what is happening in our spirit, and that activity then ignites the embers of our passion. We see an example of this when Paul discusses his spiritual son Timothy, and the effect that his heritage had upon him.

When I call to remembrance the genuine faith that is in you, which dwelt first in your grandmother Lois and your mother Eunice, and I am persuaded is in you also. Therefore I remind you to stir up the gift of God which is in you through the laying on of my hands (2 Timothy 1:5-6).

This is an incredible passage. Quick observation could have us miss its diamond of truth. Timothy had a grandmother and mother who were obviously both sincere, passionate women. Paul praises them to Timothy and reminds the young man of the women's intensity of the spirit. Somehow, that same passionate faith had been transferred into Timothy. We see here that passion is a state of being that each individual can desire and also pass down to future generations! This same passion did not lose intensity through three generations of Timothy's family!

Could we have missed a great key to bringing revival and, therefore, reformation into our cities and nations? Each revival has been built around an individual, and though many people displayed undeniable passion and often imparted it to others, they never left their passion as a heritage! They displayed passion, but were unable to leave it as an inheritance for the next generation. Thus, the passion dwindled; the intensity waned and eventually died. If we continue to build around a man and a platform, then we will never impart fully into the next generation.

In looking at Joshua's life, we see heritage passed on by Moses, his spiritual father: *"Now Joshua son of Nun was full of the spirit of wisdom, for Moses had laid his hands on him; and so the children of Israel heeded him, and did as the Lord had commanded Moses"* (Deut. 34:9). A young man who walked with Moses was one who received an impartation of passion from the old patriarch's spirit. When Joshua took over from where Moses left off, he led the nation into defeating its enemies. The older man's intensity of spirit was handed down to the younger and—even through the process of impartation—none of Moses' intensity ever vanished.

How can we build into people such passion that they will break through and bring reformation to the nations? Jesus did this with His 12 disciples, all of whom came from different backgrounds, social classes, and cultures. But he succeeded in building a group of individuals who could impact and reform the cities and nations of their day!!

Jesus did not build a ministry or platform for Himself. He was not concerned with putting a huge advertisement in the *Jerusalem Gazette,* or in having His latest praise CD go platinum! He wasn't out to win awards. Jesus was passionate for His cause, and this intensity caused a momentum in all He touched. Jesus was aware of the faults and limitations of His 12 men, but He brought the best qualities out of each one. He trained them to have a God encounter and, therefore, passed on a heritage for them to be passionate about His cause.

The only way of building passion in the Church is to lead the people into new dimensions of worship that propels them into a God encounter. Daniel was a man with one recognizable trait: He "knew God!" Today, Christian music has reached a peak, and we see song leaders replicating other famous worship leaders. With all this replication of man, we must ask ourselves, "Whom are we leading the people to have an encounter with— God or man?"

CHASE GOD AND YOU WILL,

PERCHANCE,

CAPTURE THE INTENSITY OF HIS HEART!

"Nothing great in the world has ever been accomplished without passion."
—*G.W.F. Hegel*

MY SOUL FOLLOWETH HARD AFTER THEE

(PSALM 63:8 KJV).

Chapter 5

A Messenger Is Sent

When New York City recovered from the initial trauma of the catastrophic event that left its bustling metropolis in a state of mourning, what remained were ash and steel strewn for miles where once stood two principle towers that represented a safe haven of its financial hub. With that graveyard of debris came a strong sense that America had been visited by a messenger of *evil*.

The messenger brought wickedness, destruction, and fear that had never before been felt or seen by a nation. Even the bombing of Pearl Harbor during the Second World War did not bring the same dread as conveyed by this messenger. When Pearl Harbor was attacked on December 7, 1941, the assault catapulted the nation into a state of total confusion and fear—from congressmen to normal citizens on the street. There had been major collateral damage and, of course, military casualties. America had not experienced such an attack since the burning of Washington in 1814.

Suddenly, the American people were thrown into a state that was alien to this impenetrable superpower. They felt victimized and confused, and perplexity was challenging the American psyche. For 11 months, the American people were left in this state until the national government determined to marshal its forces and retaliate! At Pearl Harbor, the target had been a military base with trained personnel accustomed to war, but "9/11" was an attack on everyday moms and dads.

41

Americans looked into the giant hole in the ground where the two towers had once been, as the endless search for bodies continued, and the death toll rose. Now, the nation was not only perplexed, but also now enraged! There is an enormous difference between an attack on military personnel trained for war, as compared to one against normal civilians accustomed to peace! A tired and grieving nation tried to piece together the puzzle of what happened that day, and more importantly, find out who was responsible.

Obviously, the nation would never be the same again. There was no safety in the place that was once a shelter from outside enemies; Americans were exposed and now vulnerable. Shortly after the attack, President George W. Bush told the bereaving nation "that terrorists would not get away with this message of evil; that the Western world must send a hard line message back; that this was unacceptable and intolerable behavior."

Whenever a message is given, then a messenger is sent to proclaim it. For every messenger sent with a message, a vessel is needed to contain that message. As we saw on September 11th, terrorists used a passenger airliner as the vessel to carry their message! God is no different. Just as America was sent a message of death, the Word of God reveals that when the Lord wanted to bring a new message, He also used a vessel as a messenger. God always sent a messenger of good to proclaim a new order and season. When Israel was under the reign of the tyrannical king Ahab, God sent a messenger to bring the nation into reform. *"Arise, go to Zarephath, which belongs to Sidon, and dwell there. See, I have commanded a widow there to provide for you"* (1 Kings 17:9).

The widow then responded to the messenger: *"As the Lord your God lives, I do not have bread, only a handful of flour in a bin, and a little oil in a jar; and, see, I am gathering a couple of sticks that I may go in and prepare it for myself and my son, that we may eat it, and die"* (1 Kings 17:12). God sent the prophet Elijah with a message of life. He had to connect to a dying widow, so as to bring the house and the nation life!

If God does not send us messengers—men and women who will save us—then we are in danger. We must learn to yield our hearts, so that we and the next generation will be preserved. Every generation has been in danger of dying to religious attitudes and mind-sets! Throughout history, denominations chose to die in dead religion, instead of receiving the messengers of God with fresh revelation, present truths, and a mandate for the future.

How many times in history have Church politics refused to embrace the new move of God, and that resistance has therefore blocked them from receiving revival? How many denominations once begun by a messenger of God sent to breathe life into people are now eons away from that original mandate? The problem is that even though these denominations once had life, they are now nothing more than a tired mausoleum for worn-out, spiritually dead people.

If this widow had refused the messenger sent by God, she would have also rejected the reformation that the nation was about to enter. Perhaps, after many days spent at the Brook Cherith being fed by ravens, the prophet's breath and body odor was less than desirable! One look at this disheveled prophet would have been enough to scare any poor, dying woman straight into eternity, without passing GO!! The Word tells us that the Lord had commanded, directed, and instructed the widow to wait for, and then receive, the prophet, who was the messenger with the message. It could have been so easy for the woman to reject the word of the Lord because she did not like the vessel carrying the message! How many times has the Church been guilty of this?

Another example of God sending a messenger to an unprepared people can be seen in the New Testament!

So it was, that while he was serving as a priest before God in the order of his division...And the whole multitude of the people was praying outside at the hour of incense. Then an angel of the Lord appeared to him, standing on the right side of the altar of incense. And when Zacharias saw him, he was troubled, and fear fell upon him. But, the angel said to him "Do not be afraid, Zacharias, for your prayer is heard" (Luke 1:8,10-13).

Here, a priest is coming into the Holy of Holies—the Presence of God—and the people outside were praying for him. Suddenly, he is met with an angel, and Zacharias is terrified. One would have to wonder whom Zacharias expected to meet, since he was entering the Holy of Holies, which is where only God dwelled!!!

God was about to bring a new move onto the earth. We should be a little lenient with Zacharias, because God had not spoken to anyone for hundreds of years (at least not that we have record of). We can assume Zacharias had no idea that he would be the first to hear God when He decided to speak again! A messenger from Heaven told Zacharias that he was to have a son called John, and that he would turn the hearts of the fathers to the children so as to make ready a people of God.

A message has been sent by a messenger, not for a person, but for a city, nation, and generations to come. Months later, another messenger comes with a message for an unlikely person.

Now in the sixth month the angel Gabriel was sent by God to a city of Galilee named Nazareth…And having come in, the angel said to her…And, behold you will conceive in your womb and bring forth a Son, and shall call His name Jesus. He will be great, and will be called the Son of the Highest; and the Lord will give Him the throne of His father David…Then Mary said to the angel, "How can this be since I do not know a man?" (Luke 1:26,28,31-32,34)

Here, the angel Gabriel is sent by God to a young woman, but the message was actually for the city. God always sends messengers, not just to a man for a man, but to a man for a city.

Even Jesus lamented over a city, *"O, Jerusalem, Jerusalem, the one who kills the prophets and stones those who are sent to her! How often I wanted to gather your children together, as a hen gathers her chicks under her wings, but you were not willing!"* (Matt. 23:37) Jesus didn't look at a temple or church, but cried out to the city; He was grieving that they had killed all the messengers sent to her!

Sadly, we have thought the be-all and end-all is Jesus' coming back for "our" church, and that great revival will mean multitudes sitting in "our" meetings, and that "our" name will be famous throughout the land. Jesus was sent to bring a city into a place of reform, and that city is His Church! Don't get me wrong; the Lord is passionate for His Church, but that is the difference—it is His Church. His passionate cause is not just "our" building that we call the church!

Reformation, new dimensions of the Spirit, and new moves of God always need an entrance point. Gabriel came in and then brought a message of the coming Messiah. So many times, we become so spiritual that we miss the obvious entrance point: ourselves! We must become like the sons of Issachar, who knew and were ready for the times and seasons of God; they were not like an unsuspecting Zacharias, who nearly died of fright upon realizing that he was the one to receive the message!

A young woman was the first to receive the seed of the Kingdom and the Son of God, even though she was a virgin; remember, both these messages were against the law in that day! Her first thought was that of her own state—as a young virgin girl who had never known a man. She didn't think of the generations to come; she thought first of herself: "How can this be? How can I do this?" For a moment, she forgot that although she couldn't, *He could*!

The angel had to position this young virgin, so that the Reformer of a city, nation, generations, and the eternal future would have an entrance through which to appear, and that entry point would be through a virgin womb. *"'For with God nothing will be impossible.' Then Mary said, 'Behold the maidservant of the Lord! Let it be to me according to your word.' And the angel departed from her"* (Luke 1:37-38).

Mary positioned herself for an impartation of the seed of the Reformer. She didn't say, "Oh, woe is me," with petitions and penitence, but said, "Look, here I am—the maidservant of the Lord." A servant has no rights; what the master proclaims, the servant agrees to do with no questions asked. A servant doesn't have an identity crisis, as the servant's identity is in his master—without the master, he is nothing. Mary didn't ask, "If it's really real, then show me another sign." Her response was, "Lord, I don't know how this can naturally happen, but show me the process." That attitude is what allowed Mary to embrace the Coming Reformer. Mary became the first person to receive Jesus, the Seed of Heaven, regardless of the personal cost!

On the other hand, Zacharias' first response was, "How will I know this is real? Show me a sign." Mary's response allowed her to continue the heritage of the Seed of Heaven, and partake in the process of birthing the Reformer. It was a father's honor for his firstborn son to be named after him, and also for the son to follow in his footsteps. Zacharias' response stole this privilege from him; his son was not named after him, but rather was called John. He did not become a priest and walk in his father's heritage; he did not eat from his father's table (John ate locusts) and did not wear his priestly clothes (John wore camel hair).

Today, we are a generation chasing signs in a belief that these will bring us into revival. But, it is signs that follow us, the reformers. As we understand this concept, then we will walk the process in divine order. Every messenger who brings a message from Heaven must find an entrance point so that Heaven can touch and change the earth. Today, let us be willing vessels, servants of God who are willing to forsake life itself to receive the Kingdom and be the messengers of God who bring reformation.

"If he has faith, the believer cannot be restrained. He betrays himself. He breaks out.

He confesses and teaches this gospel to the people at the risk of life itself."

—*Martin Luther*
(German leader of the Protestant Reformation)

LIFT UP YOUR HEADS, O YOU GATES!

LIFT UP, YOU EVERLASTING DOORS!

AND THE KING OF GLORY SHALL COME IN

(PSALM 24:9).

Chapter 6

The Day He Spoke!

Then Jesus returned in the power of the Spirit to Galilee, and news of Him went out through all the surrounding region. And He taught in their synagogues, being glorified by all. So He came to Nazareth where He had been brought up. And as His custom was, He went into the synagogue on the Sabbath day, and stood up to read. And He was handed the book of the prophet Isaiah. And when He had opened the book, He found the place where it was written: "The Spirit of the Lord God is upon Me, because He has anointed Me to preach the gospel to the poor; He has sent Me to heal the brokenhearted, to proclaim liberty to the captives and recovery of sight to the blind, to set at liberty those who are oppressed; to proclaim the acceptable year of the Lord." Then He closed the book, and gave it back to the attendant and sat down. And the eyes of all who were in the synagogue were fixed on Him. And He began to say to them, "Today this Scripture is fulfilled in your hearing" (Luke 4:14-21).

Reformation needs a strong spirit that can take a hard hit at old dogmas! We can't have reformation if we are scared to stand up for our beliefs! Reformation won't come by a casual contact, but with a strong force of the Spirit of God coming upon us! Jesus didn't mince words that day, and He didn't compromise to legalistic structures already set in place. He came to Nazareth, where He was sent by God. Even though His custom, religion, and culture was connected to a dying belief, He walked into the synagogue and positioned Himself to bring a message of reform!

Martin Luther didn't compromise when nailing his 95 Theses on the door of the church that he was once connected to. By doing so, he challenged the paradigms of the day! Walking the road to Wittenberg Church to pin his theses on the door, Luther positioned himself for challenge; he could have been stoned or killed on the walk home for being a heretic.

Jesus entered the synagogue and, as He stood up, was positioned to walk into His ministry. If we want the spirit of a reformer, then we must understand the dynamics of such positioning. In Luke 4:21, Jesus walked into temptation full of the Spirit, and then came out in power. Each temptation must not be a place to whine, groan, and cast blame. But it must become a place to get positioned for the next phase of ministry. Our purpose must become a place where we are positioned, either in the church or the secular world. Many times, we enter into temptation and—because we are overflowing with the passion of God's purpose for us—we come out of it defeated! Jesus came out in power! Don't die in the transition!!

We must constantly be reminded that temptation itself should not become our focus, but rather the dynamics of how we enter into and come out of it! At that moment, something supernatural happened in the life of Jesus; we must remember that the same supernatural "ministry" will encompass us—not for us to be self-indulgent, but to change a city, a nation, and generations to come.

Jesus knew who He was; He knew who lived within Him! He knew that He and His Father were one. He never doubted that fact for a second! *"In the beginning was the Word, and the Word was with God, and the Word was God"* (John 1:1). Jesus knew He was not only the Word of God, but was with God and was God! *"All things were made through Him, and without Him nothing was made that was made"* (John 1:3). In Colossians 3:16, the Scripture states, *"Let the Word of Christ dwell in you richly,"* or we could say it this way, "let Christ the Word dwell in you richly!" For the Word is Christ!

When Jesus positioned Himself that day in the synagogue, He stood up and spoke. He released the dynamic within Him as the Word of God; in essence, He released God. When Paul spoke to the church at Colosse, he was saying, *"Let God, the Word of creation, dwell in you richly, opulently, and abundantly so His Word is then released out of you."* It is just as Jesus declared, *"For out of the abundance of the heart the mouth speaks"* (Matt. 12:34).

John the Baptist was a messenger sent by God. He was *"the voice crying in the wilderness,"* who was releasing the Word that he was sent to declare. Remember, the Word had not been heard in those days; John had to abandon a belief system created by dogmas of the day. Before Mary entered her wilderness as a pregnant unmarried woman, the angel said, "You will conceive in your womb a son." Mary refused to focus on the religious, cultural, and political custom of the day, and instead she focused on purpose. Unlike Zacharias, she didn't ask, "How shall I know this?" or, in other words, "Show me proof of the purpose!" Mary said, "How can this be?" or rather, "Show me the process of the purpose."

Most Christians never ask God to show them the process of their purpose, but they simply sit in church for years and carry on regardless. If we do not know our purpose, then we will never know the process and will not release His Word. When the prophetic word is not released, then there is no dynamic to change the world we live in.

When Jesus stood up and spoke in the synagogue, He positioned Himself to release a new dynamic and God's mandate. He had come from Heaven, not to do His own will, but the will of He who sent Him. Jesus knew and understood His purpose and mandate; He released His purpose, and in so doing, released God Himself. Reformation never comes without there first being a divine release of His Word and Message. For only then is there a divine release of the Reformer and His Spirit of reformation.

Give unto the Lord, O you mighty ones, give unto the Lord glory and strength. Give unto the Lord the glory due to His name; worship the Lord in the beauty of holiness (Psalm 29:1-2).

We must realize that the avenue of voice is the central way of giving unto the Lord. Our voice has to give glory to the Lord and also express the beauty of the language given to us! Our language must open out the beauty of His Word, and unleash Christ Himself to the world. Let Christ the Word dwell in you richly, splendidly, and luxuriously! Paul was saying that the Christ within must settle and inhabit you, so as to reveal the beauty and splendor of Him who is Holy on every day.

I am reminded of when someone once told me that their native language—known as Afrikaans—was the language of angels. That statement left me bewildered until I understood what they meant: To them, that language had an indescribable beauty which was expressed when spoken! Within each of us is the Word of His power. That power is the dynamic to change our world, impact our cities, and reform our nations!

The voice of the Lord is over the waters; the God of glory thunders; the Lord is over many waters. The voice of the Lord is powerful; the voice of the Lord is full of majesty (Psalm 29:3-4).

His voice is what releases power. God is bound by His Word when we preach, so we must continue to preach the Word until the dimensions of Christ are expanded within people. *"Sing, O barren, you who have not borne! Break forth into singing and cry aloud… Enlarge the place of your tent…"* (Isa. 54:1-2). Enlargement comes through the voice. When we speak His Word, we open up new dimensions of the Spirit within others and ourselves.

The reason we see little growth is because we constantly speak on the same level! A woman who has never given birth would not know how to sing about the travail of birth. But here, the prophet says that as she digs deep into unknown territory within her innermost being, then enlargement comes! If we want to walk in new dimensions of Christ, we will have to explore territory that we have never been to before.

Paul said, *"...I labor in birth again until Christ is formed in you"* (Gal. 4:19). Paul had to come to an understanding of travail—one that was physically unknown to him as a male—to enable Christ and His dimensions to be formed in the Galatians. Continue to speak until His power is demonstrated and His dimensions are experienced.

THE VOICE OF THE LORD IS FULL OF MAJESTY!

The Lord's voice establishes the majesty, rule, and reign of God, and it will establish His Kingdom. When Jesus taught the disciples to pray, He said, "Thy Kingdom come." By releasing His voice and His Word, we release revelation of His Kingdom, which will break out in our lives and regions.

We will never bring back the government of God unless we have a revelation of the power of releasing His Voice through His Word. We must teach people to pray more than just "bless me" prayers! Every disciple must be trained to pray governmental prayers; these can only be prayed after a disciple has come to a place of self-government. God's Kingdom is always advancing, so our prayers must be advancing also! Most Christians and churches pray just to get God to move: "Oh God, send us revival" is not a governmental prayer!

Pray His Word to accelerate what He is already doing in our midst! Most churches are journaling what God is doing today, instead of speaking His Word and causing momentum into tomorrow. We must start to see *Who* we have within us. When our concept of who He is becomes corrected and adjusted, then who we are in Him will be accurate.

The prodigal son didn't understand his inheritance and heritage; he really had no understanding of who his father was. This passage has been interpreted evangelically. Now, let's look at it in the light of reformation. *"And the younger [son] of them* *said to his father, 'Father, give me the portion of the goods that falls to me.' So he divided to them his **livelihood**"* (Luke 15:12, emphasis added).

Many of us have heard this preached that the father gave his son the inheritance that was due to him. How can this be? Is that an accurate explanation? Think about it. First, the verse says the father divided his *livelihood*. Our livelihood is totally different from our inheritance! Our livelihood is our living, our business, or the earnings from a job. Second, Luke 15:20 reads, *"And he arose and came to his father...."* If the father had divided the full inheritance to his sons, then where did the younger son come back too? Perhaps the father had moved to a retirement village or a nice unit by the sea? Absurd as that may sound, if the inheritance had been divided in half, then the father would not still be living on that same land! Land was always the inheritance. *"For all the land which you see I give to you and your descendants forever"* (Gen. 13:15).

We know that the prodigal son came back to the same place, the same land, because the older son says, *"Lo, these many years I have been serving you..."* (Luke 15:29). The elder lad asserts that while the younger son was away, he had been working his father's land. Feeling the arrangement to be unfair, the older son refused to come to the party. When the prodigal returned, he came back to his father—and not just his father's belongings—because experience had changed the young man's character.

Above all, the prodigal trusted his father's character! Even though he believed that he had lost the spirit of sonship (as Noah's and Eli's sons had), the young man knew that his father would take him back and feed him. If the Church does not stop coming for what God has, instead of who He is, we will never see reformation. Parents knows that their child doesn't have to ask for food, clothes, and adequate shelter. Only in an absurd, dysfunctional family would a child have to ask for daily food! This is the place where some of us have come with the Heavenly Father: I must come to Him alone, not to His belongings. I find contentment and peace in this place of overwhelming trust.

Every time we preach His Word, His voice is released and His Kingdom must break out. When no Word is preached, then the atmosphere falls into a place of exhaustion, laziness, and darkness, and the land itself enters a time of barrenness.

Lucifer's sin catapulted the earth into a place of darkness and led to the fall of one-third of all angels. Darkness covered the face of the deep. Lucifer was Heaven's worshiper who covered the throne of God. Ezekiel 28 states that he was the cherub who covered, and that workmanship and timbrels were prepared for him on the day of his creation. When lucifer fell, the creation that existed before mankind also collapsed. Suddenly, Heaven's worshiper was tainted and reduced to a fallen, decaying being. Lucifer could now only produce sin and death, which were qualities of his character. *"For the wages of sin is death"* (Rom. 6:23).

Sin epitomized satan's nature, and now that sin was producing a penalty of death! When worship is removed, then, consequently, God-given structure is also removed. In the Old Testament, every army was structured by the worshipers. Removing worship removes structure, which, in turn, and removes order. When structure is removed, only darkness and chaos reign in its place. God's spoken Word was the substance that recreated the earth and brought it back into godly, governmental order. Sadly, we have replaced God's structure with a legalist form of religious structure based on position and titles, instead of on worship and intimacy, which is God's true divine order!

God said, *"Let there be light,"* and light came into being! With that, His Kingdom in the heavens was now revealed and established as substance. When His Word is declared, the Kingdom is manifested on the earth. *"You will also declare a thing, and it will be established for you"* (Job 22:28). When we declare *"His kingdom come"* in our cities, the Word that is being declared causes a shift in the heavens, which will then be established in our midst. When the Kingdom manifests in people's lives, His majestic behavior soon follows. That majestic behavior is where His love, grace, mercy, and righteousness is recognizable in the Church's life.

THE VOICE OF THE LORD BREAKS THE CEDARS

The Lord's voice has the power to transcend any human strength. The cedar is one of the sturdiest trees, and its root system digs deep into the soil; as the tree grows, it develops hardy branches in a tall and powerful tree. These trees can withstand the greatest adversity of weather conditions. The voice of the Lord will break the hardest of hearts.

The voice of the Lord is full of majesty. The voice of the Lord breaks the cedars, Yes, the Lord splinters the cedars of Lebanon. He makes them also skip like a calf, Lebanon and Sirion like a young wild ox. The voice of the Lord divides the flames of fire. The voice of the Lord shakes the wilderness; the Lord shakes the Wilderness of Kadesh. The voice of the Lord makes the deer give birth, and strips the forests bare; and in His temple everyone says, "Glory!" The Lord sat enthroned at the Flood, and the Lord sits as King forever. The Lord will give strength to His people; the Lord will bless His people with peace (Psalm 29:4-11).

The hardest human heart or will can be disintegrated in mere moments by His voice. Saul (Paul) was adamant in his relentless persecution of the early Church. On a Damascus road, Saul was still breathing threats and murder against the disciples. His mission was to imprison as many (Christian) men and women as possible. Suddenly, Saul fell to the ground when a bright light shone on him. A voice said to him, "Why are you persecuting Me?" Blinded by the Light of the World, Saul suddenly transformed in a moment. His hardened heart was splintered by the Lord's voice and a man reappeared in a transformed state.

Even though the Lord's voice will break and shatter a hard human heart, He will never leave it in pieces. He will reshape the man or woman to skip like a calf. No matter how obstinate and inflexible a human heart may be, the Lord never leaves it broken; He will cause it to be lively and full of freedom and joy with a spirit full of exuberance.

The voice of the Lord is able to harness a young, raw spirit and connect it to His own Spirit. This will, in turn, cause the raw spirit to be transformed into a vessel full of potential. The wild ox is an animal of either male or female gender. The animal represents how the Lord's voice will remove every earthly restraint and debris of dead religion, so that a man of God is unable to be held back from reaching his full potential and destiny!

A young ox is one with a great destiny and a full future ahead of him! The ox speaks of the ability of an animal to work hard. Even with a day full of tiresome field work, it will not relent until its purpose is fulfilled—no matter what hardships may be encountered. Psalm 110:3 says, *"Your people shall be volunteers in the day of Your power."* Like the ox, His people will see purpose ahead and volunteer to fulfill the work ahead that is the Master's purpose. The wild ox will skip like a young calf with youthful exuberance and go to the highest peaks of destiny.

THE VOICE OF THE LORD DIVIDES THE FLAMES OF FIRE

The Lord's voice will bring fire to devour what needs to be consumed, and, from that, will divide and cleanse what can be saved. We must become firebrands in His hand. Our words must be strong, courageous, and full of fire. But fire is not necessarily volume—it is where intensity in our spirit is like a flame in our mouths. The prophet Jeremiah said, *"But His word was in my heart like a burning fire shut up in my bones; I was weary of holding it back…"* (Jer. 20:9). After talking with the risen Lord, two disciples said, after talking to Him, *"Did not our heart burn within us while He talked with us on the road…"* (Luke 24:32).

As we lift our voice to speak His Word, then our words must be like a fire that has been shut up in our hearts; it burns into people to cleanse and remove all impurities from their souls. Fire will cause us to become soft and pliable in nature. For gold to be purified and shaped, it must go through the fire to remove its impurities. As His fire burns us, we are transformed by His divine nature, and our nature becomes like His.

When building an altar to God before the prophets of Baal, Elijah put wood on the fire. *"And he put the wood in order, cut the bull in pieces, and laid it on the wood, and said, 'Fill four waterpots with water, and pour it on the burnt sacrifice and the wood...The fire of God fell and consumed the burnt sacrifice, and the wood..."* (1 Kings 18:33,38). Wood speaks of our humanity; His divinity consumes it. Fire consumes our attitudes, motives, and agendas.

THE VOICE OF THE LORD SHAKES THE WILDERNESS

A wilderness is an impenetrable place. The voice of the Lord will impact the most impossible situation. Ezekiel was taken to a place full of death—a valley full of dried bones! God told him to lift his voice to reshape the landscape and restructure society! A valley of dead, dry bones was suddenly a living, breathing army, who God said was now the house and nation of Israel, *"I, the Lord, have spoken it and performed it..."* (Ezek. 37:14). God puts us into nations to do more than just live in those societies, but to reshape and redesign them! Let our voices carry His breath and fire—the same breath and fire that said, "Light, be," and restructured the earth.

THE VOICE OF THE LORD MAKES THE DEER GIVE BIRTH

The voice of the Lord will cause the seeds to reproduce by His power. His voice causes the reproductive cycle in the deer and throughout nature itself. His voice is life, releases life, and causes the reproductive cycle of the living to continue!

Nothing hidden will be kept in darkness; His voice will wash out the darkest corner of the darkest forest, and bring it into light. Even what is hidden in human hearts will be brought into the light by His voice! *"For there is nothing covered that will not be revealed, and hidden that will not be known"* (Matt. 10:26). *"Therefore judge nothing before the time, until the Lord comes, who will both bring to light the hidden things of darkness and reveal the counsels of the hearts..."* (1 Cor. 4:5).

AND IN HIS TEMPLE EVERYONE SAYS, "GLORY!"

Suddenly, His voice causes His people to cry out for His Glory! Now it is not His voice calling out anymore, but His people crying out to Him. His voice has stirred intensity in His temple, and His people cry out to embrace Him. Everybody is united as one—there is unity and agreement. Jesus said that when two or more are in agreement, then their Father in Heaven will do what they ask. When His people cry out and simultaneously declare *"Glory!,"* then His earth will be filled with His Glory!

THE LORD SAT ENTHRONED AT THE FLOOD

When God brought a flood on humanity in the Book of Genesis, He first gave Noah the commandment; when Noah did all that He commanded, then the Flood came to pass. God spoke His word first, and then fulfilled His promise. God spoke, and then Noah released the word that God had given him for his generation. In Heaven, the water was held by His voice; if God does not have a man in which to download what He is saying, then there is no fulfillment of divine promise. God always uses men and women to speak His divine purpose into the earth. God will not bring judgment where a man or woman has first brought His Word of purpose.

AND THE LORD SITS AS KING FOREVER

His Kingdom will reign forever and ever. There is no end to His Kingdom—it is unfathomable and beyond depth. Paul cried out that He might know the depth, width, and breadth of His Kingdom. God rules eternally; the closer we search out, the farther away He is! Our souls must find Him and eternally chase Him.

THE LORD WILL GIVE STRENGTH TO HIS PEOPLE

"And Ezra opened the book in the sight of all the people, for he was standing above all the people; and when he opened it, all the people stood up..." (Neh. 8:5). Then, Ezra, who was the priest and scribe, said to all the people, *"For the joy of the Lord is your strength"* (Neh. 8:10). The people likened reading His Word to the voice of God speaking. In exuberance, they stood and rejoiced at the sound. His voice will activate faith and joy, and will cause us to be strengthened to fulfill His purpose—even when it's not yet seen with our natural eyes!

THE LORD WILL BLESS HIS PEOPLE WITH PEACE

"Blessed are the peacemakers, for they shall be called sons of God" (Matt. 5:9). God's people are blessed, empowered to prosper with peace, and then changed from His people to His sons! The Book of Romans states that all of creation eagerly waits the revealing of the sons of God. His sons will carry His voice and transform creation, which is not just awaiting liberty, but also to hear the voice of Him who will set it free.

When Isaiah stood in the temple of Heaven (in Isaiah 6:1-4), he saw the temple's structure shaken by the Lord's voice. His dynamic of voice changed the structure of God's dwelling place. The temple became a house; the place of visitation became the place of habitation. Hearing the Lord's voice shake the structures of His abode in Heaven, Isaiah suddenly saw the King! Until that point, his eyes had seen the Lord, Heaven, the temple, and even the angelic beings surrounding the Throne. But suddenly the voice of the King revealed the Kingdom of God, and Isaiah opened his eyes and saw the King of Kings for the first time!

If we want to change religious structures of our denominational and church boundaries, impact our cities, and revolutionize our nations, then we must listen to His voice, raise our voices together with Him, and allow His Word to flood our cities! Let us allow the Lord to open our eyes, so that we can see the King and His Kingdom as never before!

AND THE POSTS OF THE DOOR WERE SHAKEN BY THE VOICE OF HIM WHO CRIED OUT,

AND THE HOUSE WAS FILLED WITH SMOKE.

SO I SAID,

"WOE IS ME, FOR I AM UNDONE! …FOR MY EYES HAVE SEEN THE KING"

(ISAIAH 6:5).

Chapter 7

Who Is This Man?

Hundreds of years before Jesus was born, the prophet Isaiah (in his 74th prophecy) revealed how the coming Messiah would appear and what He would do. The day Jesus started His public ministry, He stood up in the synagogue and quoted Isaiah's prophecy. After quoting it, He finished by saying, "Today this scripture has been fulfilled in your midst." Now, the words on everyone's lips that day, as they watched His every move in amazement and awe was, "Who is this man?"

The Spirit of the Lord God is upon Me; because the Lord has anointed Me to preach good tidings to the poor; He has sent Me to heal the brokenhearted, to proclaim liberty to the captives, and the opening of the prison to those who are bound (Isaiah 61:1).

His first words that day were like a dynamite blast that decimated hard rocks of religion and tradition in every person's soul, and shattered formerly held beliefs. When the dust cleared, and all eyes gazed at the Man (known by many as the carpenter's son), did they truly perceive who was standing before them?

THE SPIRIT OF THE LORD GOD IS UPON ME

What an astonishing statement, and it's one that we have overlooked. The Church has majored on the fact that just as He was anointed, so too are we. Yet, we missed the most powerful fact, which was, that who He is also resides in us! Jesus stood before these learned men and said, "His Spirit is upon Me!" What then did He actually mean? What was Jesus declaring that day to His generation and the generations to come? We know that He is the Son of God, but here He stated that "the Spirit of the Lord" was upon Him.

The Church has thoroughly dissected First Corinthians 12–14 in regards to the gifts of the Spirit. Most of us have come to a place where we are comfortable with giftings that operate in our lives. But Jesus didn't say "the gifts of the Spirit are upon Me," but rather that "the Spirit of the Lord is upon Me!"

Christianity must not be all about having gifts operating in our life, but should also include having an increased dimension of the Spirit breaking out in our life. When we allow the gifts to operate, then we allow the Giver to offer us, at any random time, part of something He is. When we allow dimensions of the Spirit to break out within us, then who He is becomes part of our internal configuration, pattern, and nature. We need to understand dimensions of His Spirit before we can ever expect a reformer's spirit to break out in our nations.

Firstly, we must establish who the Spirit of the Lord is. When Jesus made that statement that day, He wasn't just giving them a Charismatic message. We hear people say, "Oh I feel in my spirit this," or "I feel the Lord is saying that!" Let's stop that and start being accurate! What exactly do we feel? If we rely on "feelings," then we will be inaccurate in our thought and behavior patterns. We either hear God speak in our spirit or not.

Learn, as Jesus did, to hear and to do! Not once did Jesus stand before the multitudes and say, "I feel God may be saying for Me to heal some of you today!" That's preposterous! He said, "I do what I hear My Father tell Me." If we want to become precise in our internal configuration, then we must see, hear, and do!

The Spirit of the Lord is the dimension of the triune Godhead that conveys the Lordship of Christ and the Government and Kingdom of God into our lives. Unless the dimension of the Spirit of the Lord breaks out within us, then we will not see His Kingdom upon us! *"Therefore, since we are* receiving *a kingdom which cannot be shaken..."* (Heb. 12:28). We must receive His Kingdom—its rules, values, honor, integrity, and truth—or we will be revealing a religious system and not His Church. God's Church is to openly show and declare His Kingdom, and not religious systems!

"But when they believed Philip as he preached the things concerning the kingdom of God and the name of Jesus Christ..." (Acts 8:12). Philip not only preached Jesus Christ, but also the Kingdom of God! Today, the Church has preached the gospel of Jesus—which is a gospel of salvation—extremely well. But when there is a breaking out of apostles, that's when we will see an explosion of the Kingdom! The gospel of salvation is different from the gospel of Kingdom, although you cannot have one without the other. When the gospel of salvation is preached, then war breaks out. But when we preach Kingdom, then Heaven invades! Salvation marches us into enemy territory, so that we can to win back what was stolen. But we want to do more than win back the spoils; we must invade enemy territory and declare total victory! Rule, reign, and conquer!

WAS HE AN APOSTLE?

Jesus is the Apostle of our faith; He came to declare the Kingdom of God. So, what is an apostle and what is apostolic teaching? When John the Baptist spoke of Jesus in relation to himself, he proclaimed, *"One mightier than I is coming, whose sandal strap I am not worthy to loose. He will baptize you with the Holy Spirit and fire"* (Luke 3:16). The one he declared was to come was Jesus, who was and is the great apostle of our faith. Scripture tells us to consider Jesus, the Apostle and High Priest of our confession. If Jesus is the great Apostle, then what He taught and how He behaved should be a pattern for us to follow.

The writer of Hebrews tells us that Moses was faithful in his entire house as a servant, but there was one who built the house and who was a son over the house. A servant does not build the house and is never over the house. Only a father or son can build a house and, therefore, be over the household. Therefore, the foundational truth of apostolic teaching would be building a house, not a "corporate church" or religious structure.

Today, many are building mega-churches and enjoying growing membership. Let's be honest: Any organization has members who vote usually with their feet! Members are like slaves because they are not sons, and slaves are bought and sold by the highest bidder! Only a house and a family have sons! An apostle does not have fervor just to grow numerically, but to birth sons in the house and Kingdom. The apostle Paul once said, *"My little children, for whom I labor in birth again until Christ is formed in you"* (Gal. 4:19).

"And they continued steadfastly in the apostles' doctrine and fellowship" (Acts 2:42). Apostles are men connected to God, who know Him intimately through a divine encounter that allows them to form God's life and Kingdom in us. In the days of Acts, the apostles did not have a Bible in written form, so they had to be intimate with God and then relay to people what they heard from God. They discerned what God was doing and how He was moving, and then kept progressive revelation, which caused forward momentum.

Peter stood on the brink of tradition and culture and on the verge of the Kingdom of Heaven breaking out on the earth. He brought clarity to the people by proclaiming what God was doing in their midst. Peter did not argue whether there was a theological doctrine, or perhaps a confirmation of this elsewhere; he was able keep momentum of God's activity in their midst. So often when God moves today, He comes in unexpected ways that theologians and teachers want to explain away. Meanwhile, apostles will stand and declare that to be a move of God and will then implore people to move with Him.

When John the Baptist said, *"Prepare the way of the Lord; make His paths straight,"* (Matt. 3:3), he created an entrance point for a move of God. We need apostles today who can create an avenue for the Kingdom of Heaven to invade earth. Every move must have forerunners and disciples. The forerunners create the path and then direct the disciples. A disciple cannot become a disciple unless a mentor trains him to become a disciple. Disciples must be discipled in a modern move of God, and not in what God was doing yesterday. They must be taught to search for God passionately! Remember God is not lost, but often we lose our direction.

Paul found some disciples as he passed through Ephesus and asked if they had received the Holy Spirit. They answered, "We have not heard there is a Holy Spirit!" Were these men saved? Yes, but unfortunately were disciples of an old move—John's baptism. They needed an apostle to bring clarity to their belief, upgrading them into the now move of God.

Apostolic teaching is shown in Acts 20:32, *"So now brethren, I* [the apostle] *commend you to God and to the word of His grace, which is able to build you up and give you an inheritance among all those who are sanctified."* These men were not just having church, but were sharing the Life of God that had been formed within them and each other. Today, the word "fellowship" is misused—it's used for everything from fellowship teas to fellowship barbeques. But we must understand that fellowship is not centered around food; in actuality, it has nothing to do with food.

So, it's erroneous to infer that eating a meal together means having fellowship. Fellowship builds relationship, and it's where we allow the Word of God within us to be partaken of by those relating to us. *"If you extend your soul to the hungry and satisfy the afflicted soul…"* (Isa. 58:10). True fellowship is not only where we share food, but also where we become the food for another's soul. This is certainly a new and different level of our understanding of "fellowship."

In the light of the Word, we are to examine ourselves. We have taught people to be sin-conscious instead of God-conscious. Communion has become a place of "Woe is me," instead of "Where am I in relation to where He is?" Who He is—that's what allows me to know who I am today! Looking at sin keeps me in a place of individuality and isolation. But when I keep my gaze on who He is and who I am in Him, that is when I stay focused on His Body. Of course, we are not saying that we should not judge ourselves, because that would be foolish.

"And they continued steadfastly in the apostles' doctrine and fellowship, in the breaking of bread, and in prayers" (Acts 2:42). They did not pray "it's all about me" prayers. Today's church is continually focused on itself. Let us not be naïve to say that God doesn't meet our needs; of course, He does. But if we continue focusing on our needs, we will never rise up into the position of our calling. God is our Father, so we don't have to daily ask Him, or even worse, confess until hoarse that "I have a car, house, boat, and dog." These all belong to me as a son of God! It is time that we rise up and prayed governmental prayers to release God's will and purpose in our nations.

When apostles start to break out, that's when the Church will become established on God's government and not that of man. If God's government is not brought back into the Church, then His Kingdom is not manifest on the earth. This is why evangelists must connect to the apostolic; if not, people will get saved, but His Kingdom will not be breaking out in people's lives. Remember that Philip preached the gospel of salvation *and* the Kingdom!

If the church is not preaching Kingdom as well as salvation, then it is in danger of becoming religious and controlling. Programs to get people saved are rarely successful long-term. Therefore, if the Kingdom is not being preached, then it will not manifest in the lives of converts, disciples, and mentors. What we use to gain people is what we must use to get them to remain. When people come because of a program, then we must keep the programs to keep the people. We must connect people to Heaven, not to a human.

Often, we see worship leaders turn into an all-singing, all-dancing worship machine just to try to get people to worship! If a worship leader has to do "gymnastics" to keep people focused, then he had better think twice about his mentality! This is a symptom of a performance mentality that, sadly, breeds performing believers who are not connected to God! Ministers must increase not only in gifting, but also in the spirit dimensions. We hear so much about "going to the next level." But, in actuality, all we are doing is increasing in knowledge and "anointing" of our gifting!

That day in the temple, when Jesus said that "the Spirit of the Lord…was upon [Him]," what was He actually declaring? The answer is in the Book of Isaiah, but we must first come to an understanding of the prophet's words.

There shall come forth a Rod from the stem of Jesse, and a Branch shall grow out of his roots. The Spirit of the Lord shall rest upon Him, the Spirit of wisdom and understanding, the Spirit of counsel and might, the Spirit of knowledge and of the fear of the Lord (Isaiah 11:1-2).

When the Spirit of the Lord is present, it brings liberty. Liberty is freedom, and free people are not religious people. We see people quote this Scripture, and you sometimes wonder if they truly believe what they are quoting! People controlled by a religious, manipulating system are anything but free. Striving to attend meeting after meeting until you are burned out is not freedom. Being frightened to leave a system for fear of losing your life, marriage, or job is not freedom— it's a sinister form of control.

If a pastor or leader is not secure in his call and position as a son, then he will continue to control people out of an ongoing fear that they might leave. Many leaders do not even recognize this control, even though they preach against it. Yet, people are kept in bondage by having to attend meeting after meeting. Oftentimes, pastors will create an underlying sense of fear in a church; so much so, that people become trapped in a culture of dread—they fear that to disobey the church's unwritten culture means walking out of God's will. Our church culture should be one of liberty: Where the Spirit of the Lord is there is liberty! We must understand that liberty is not coming out from under the cover of authority. But control and authority are two radically different concepts!

The prophet said, *"The Spirit of the Lord shall rest upon Him [the Spirit of Lordship]"* (Isa. 11:2). He then goes on to speak of the seven dimensions of the Spirit of the Lord that will manifest on the One who comes from the root of Jesse. When Jesus declared that *"the Spirit of the Lord is upon Me,"* He meant that the sevenfold dimension of the Spirit of God was operating through Him!

The prophet Isaiah said that the coming Messiah would function in a sixth-fold dimension of the Spirit. But in Ephesians, the apostle Paul says that the Church, or the Body of Christ—which is the fullness, or completeness of Jesus Christ—would function in the seventh dimension. Paul speaks to us through one of the greatest dialogues, which is now taken as a foundation for prayer in a believer's life. Paul adds the extra, or seventh, dimension from Isaiah's revelation:

> *...that the God of our Lord Jesus Christ, the Father of glory, may give to you the* spirit of wisdom, and [Spirit of] revelation in the [Spirit of] knowledge of Him, *the eyes of your* [Spirit of] understanding *being enlightened...and what is the exceeding greatness of His* power [Spirit of might] *toward us who believe...* (Ephesians 1:17-19, emphasis added).

In the Book of Revelation, John, while on the Isle of Patmos speaks of *"a Lamb as though it had been slain, having seven horns and seven eyes, which are the seven Spirits of God sent out into all the earth"* (Rev. 5:6). Of course, we know that there are *not* seven Spirits of God, but seven dimensions of the same Spirit.

What are these seven dimensions of the Spirit upon Jesus when He walked the earth? Is it possible that these dimensions can be in the life of every believer? If we could walk in these dimensions (instead of playing on the outer limits of our giftings), would we start to see the Church walk in the dimension of fullness of Christ? Perhaps this is why the temple in the outer court was biggest: because most Christians don't want to get too close to the fire! Let's be the ones who dare to walk in!

THE SPIRIT OF WISDOM

The Spirit of Wisdom causes us to become accurate in every part of our internal makeup, personality, character, and mentality. If we do not have accuracy in our walk, then we will not be able to build correctly and accurately. This dimension of the Spirit of God brings us to a place of maturity.

This is different from the Word of Wisdom (see 1 Cor. 12), which is where we have a fragment of God's wisdom for His future plans and purposes. The Spirit of Wisdom is not the same: It is where we can see into a situation, bring a person's life into a place of accuracy, and break old mind-sets and wrong internal patterns to allow for new ones.

Many people are growing in their walk with God, but still have wrong internal patterns. So often, we see Christians (and even ministers) who look great on Sunday, but their personal lives are a wreck Monday through Saturday. Often, these men and women have highly developed gifts of the Spirit, so where does the problem lie?

When Jesus told the disciples to "tarry till the Holy Spirit comes," 120 of them were obedient. The Feast of Pentecost was going on down on the streets below. Many were making the pilgrimage into the city with their families to continue a cultural norm handed down by religious leaders for centuries. When the Holy Spirit came and a new move overflowed into the streets, Peter brought accuracy to what was happening, by declaring his famous statement.

Only the Spirit of Wisdom can break old thought patterns that have caused immovable mind-sets and bring blueprints to build new structures. We cannot win a religious war with theological arguments; we must change people's paradigms! Old thinking encompasses old behavior patterns. Religious thinking breeds religious behavior patterns! Apostles must have this dimension of the Spirit operating in their life so as to build what God is doing today in the Church and in an individual's life.

THE SPIRIT OF UNDERSTANDING

The Spirit of Understanding must not be confused with general knowledge, spiritual knowledge, or known facts about a person or circumstance. The Spirit of Understanding allows the Word of God to be opened effectively, to bring fresh understanding of what God is doing today and, therefore, allow believers to renew their minds. When Paul was writing the Book of Romans, he had just brought understanding of the Word from the Old Testament; now, he exhorted the Church that renewing their minds would bring transformation.

Although we hear a good preaching message, it is often not what the Holy Spirit is saying to the Church today, but is just a man's pet doctrine. We must give people understanding of how to use the Word of God to accomplish what it is set out to do! *"For the word of God is living and powerful, and sharper than any two-edged sword, piercing even to the division of the soul and spirit, and joints and marrow, and is a discerner of the thoughts and intents of the heart"* (Heb. 4:12). The Word of God is able to pierce between the flesh, soul, and spirit of man.

THE SPIRIT OF COUNSEL

This is not counseling! We have seen the Church take the world's methods and bring them into the sanctuary. Counseling is a low-level use of the anointing, and it's a concept taken from the world to suit our belief system. The Church must never become a replacement for a psychiatrist! Many enjoy inner healing either as a patient or a counselor because of wrong internal patterns that have not been effectively dealt with. Having people return to counselors for advice allows them to become dependent and find another person (other than God) as a source of answers. To keep returning to a counselor is usually a sign of dependency on the part of the one seeking counsel, and often on the counselor for a sense of identity! This behavior pattern will breed immaturity. These individuals hide within the systems themselves and will often disrupt people, undermine leadership, and subvert the purpose of the entire house.

This is a Charismatic doctrine, and churches need to remove people from this dependency or else the church will remain unhealthy and never grow. Any dependency in a church—whether it is the need to minister or receive ministry—is totally unhealthy and needs to be starved so that people learn to find God for themselves. Most churches need to dismantle this type of ministry until it is clearly detected if any unhealthy behavior pattern is being produced. Counsel should be very quick and not drawn out—it is to inspire and open up people's destiny, so they can walk toward it on their own feet. If a person continually uses a crutch, he causes his muscles to weaken and soon they are rendered ineffective. Faith is the same; if it is continually unproductive, it soon becomes weak and ineffective.

The Spirit of Counsel facilitates a person not only to get back on the road to destiny, but often to help them find that road again. People must be given the mind of Christ (not the mind of the counselor), the way of the Lord, and the right path to walk in, which is not necessarily the easiest to follow. During the past 20 years, there has been an upsurge of so-called Christian counseling methods; some of it is based on psychology and some is based on downright stupidity.

Counseling must never analyze a problem so as to agree with the consciousness! This is psychology! The Spirit of Counsel will tell us what to do in light of His Word, and not what our psyche agrees with. Most counseling is not what is right, but is what people want to hear. The pains of someone's past is not the point; the fact is that the Spirit of the Lord shows us our destiny, and not our history. Therefore, counsel should be done in godly divine order; it is to inspire and open up a person's destiny so a person can walk toward it on their own two feet.

Deliverance and inner healing does have a valid place, so we must not remove it all together. But we must look at unhealthy patterns that often pollute systems in the Church. Having done that, we must then start this ministry afresh, with new dynamics in place. The writer of Hebrews told us to put our past behind and to look forward; we are to stop peering in the rearview mirror of life, but gaze ahead diligently to Jesus. So, why are we dredging up someone's sorry past? Why do we still use this Charismatic model? If we are to build with people, then we must starve this Charismatic model and teach people to go to God, not to a mediator called a counselor.

Again, there is an upsurge of the deliverance move where people spend hours on the floor trying to get delivered of everything. We all have a past—an event classed as deeply upsetting, intensely grievous or, perhaps, even heinous—but to continue focusing on these events keeps us locked into a victim/survival mentality. Recognize that everyone has a past, but people who are not allowed to look at tomorrow will forever live in an unproductive, dependent, victim mentality. Let them know these words: They survived and now live, for there is a tomorrow!

We do not want people to just survive—we want them to have life! We are to be overcomers. Yet, people are clinging to a pattern of constant defeat by regurgitating the past. The world often overcomes better than the Church; we have developed a Charismatic doctrine that means our counselors keep members in a place of dependence. Don't counsel someone back to the past, but help get them in line with a future and a God-given destiny! Pastors must possess this dimension of the Holy Spirit so as not to get burned out. Remember, it is the Spirit of Counsel who reveals His divine purposes, plans, and destiny for His sons, and also reveals His divine counsel for their lives.

THE SPIRIT OF KNOWLEDGE

The Spirit of Knowledge is not the same as the gift of the Word of Knowledge, which is a fragment of God's eternal knowledge (past, present, or future) about a person or circumstance. The Spirit of Knowledge is the ability to hear the secret things of God. Prophets should be walking in this dimension. The Lord reveals all His secrets to the prophets before He does anything (see Amos 3:7). So, in times of intensity, we need this dimension of His Spirit to direct our download from Heaven.

Jesus said, *"And I know that His command is everlasting life. Therefore, whatever I speak, just as the Father has told Me, so I speak"* (John 12:50). This is the power of knowing. Jesus didn't feel, sense, or think He heard His Father; His intimate relationship— based on knowledge of His own identity as the Son—allowed Him to hear accurately and then do in power and authority!

Jesus says, *"At that day* [that is today] *you will know that I am in My Father, and you in Me, and I in you"* (John 14:20). We must come into this dimension of the Spirit of Knowledge, which leads us to know who we are in Him. If we do not understand that our identity is not in our works and our giftings, but in our sonship, then we will never understand that our identity lies in Him. As a result, we will try to fill the void with other external pursuits, such programs or agendas. The Church is going through an identity crisis in trying to make programs that give us an identity; it must return to being in Him and the personal knowledge that "I have an identity because I am His son."

THE SPIRIT OF MIGHT

This is where miraculous works of God break out. The Spirit of Might can be seen when the sovereign work of God arrests a situation and brings liberty and wholeness. People today are crying out for gifts of the working of miracles. But when we desire to reform a nation, we need more than one miracle; the Spirit of Might must be manifested throughout the Body of Christ. The Spirit of the Lord was upon Jesus—not just the gifts of the Spirit every now and then.

When the Body of Christ walks in a dimension of the Spirit of Might, then the miraculous will become the norm and the supernatural will become natural. On the Day of Pentecost, Peter stood up and repeated what the prophet Joel declared hundreds of years before: *"I will pour out of My Spirit on all flesh...I will show wonders in heaven above and signs in the earth beneath..."* (Acts 2:17,19). That is the Spirit of Might in manifestation. When a nation sees reformation, then this dimension of the Spirit of God will break forth like never before! The Spirit of Might brings a breakout of the Kingdom of God into people's lives.

THE SPIRIT OF THE FEAR OF THE LORD

The Spirit of the Fear of the Lord is also known as the Spirit of Awe. When manifested, it brings people to a place of recognizing the Fear of the Lord in their midst. This Spirit must not be confused with human fear and control; so often pastors are found guilty of saying, "If you leave my church or organization, then you will die, or your ministry will be in disgrace." This is nothing more than fear and manipulation! God is the Author and Finisher of a man or woman's life, not men—no matter how anointed they are! Often, prophets will come into a church, make a negative prophecy, and put people in fear and trembling so that they believe the prophet. Prophets must prophesy the positive, not the negative. Occasionally, of course, a prophet will warn about a situation that he is unaware of (that he could have only learned from God), and then people become angry because they do not want to hear that!

Some years ago, a prophet spoke over a large continent that the area was about to be cut in half by God's wrath, and that one-half would fall into the sea. Of course, the obvious question was, "Which half?" Since both halves have good men and women living on them who are God's children, which ones would He propose to kill? Another prophetic word was that God was about to judge a nation for its atrocities during a world war, and that the people must repent. Again, we can ask the obvious: "When will the judgment finish? How much repentance is enough?" These sorts of words put people in a place of fear and then into a mentality of works.

The Fear of the Lord draws people closer to motivate them into a place of intimacy with the Beloved; it does not drive them away

76

to be separate from Him out of terror. The Fear of the Lord is meant to bring us to a place of God-consciousness through His presence. *"Then fear came upon every soul, and many wonders and signs were done through the apostles"* (Acts 2:43). A following verse notes that many thousands were saved. This dimension of the Spirit will produce and manifest grace, so we can recognize an apostolic anointing through the Fear of the Lord. An apostolic nature is one where great grace is clearly visible upon the person, and it allows him to function in this dimension.

In Acts 5, Ananias and Sapphira lied to the Holy Spirit and fell down dead in a meeting. This certainly put a bit of a damper on the gathering. Did Peter turn to the choir and shout "sing louder," or call for the deacons to "take up an offering fast!" No, after a funeral service *"great fear came upon all the church and upon all who heard these things. And through the hands of the apostles many signs and wonders were done among the people"* (Acts 5:11-12). This is true apostolic behavior! That verse does not tell us only of healings and miracles alone, but also speaks of signs and wonders. The Spirit of Awe is not about how inspirational the sermon was, but is concerned with how His presence came!

When God inhabits the praises of His people, then we will see the Spirit of Awe manifest. Inhabiting the praises of His people is not where we have a positive confession about Him being there, but is when the Father makes His abode among us. During every revival, when God's manifested presence was visible, people would cry out because the Spirit of Fear (of the Lord) was evident. *The Spirit of the Fear of the Lord is the Spirit of Revival.*

THE SPIRIT OF REVELATION

Isaiah 11 speaks of how Jesus manifested the six dimensions of the Spirit of God. But in Ephesians, when Paul prays to God for that church, he says, *"the Father of glory, may give to you the spirit of wisdom and revelation"* (Eph. 1:17). The Spirit of Revelation came to the Church after Jesus died and rose again.

Remember, the number six represents "man," and seven represents "perfection." When Jesus came to earth He was the "Son of Man" as well as the Son of God. *"The body of Christ, till we all come to the unity of the faith and the knowledge of the Son of God, to a perfect man, to the measure of the stature of the fullness of Christ"* (Eph. 4:12-13). The full dimensions of Christ are now fulfilled in and through His Body!

When the Spirit of Revelation is revealed to us, He then will download the purposes and plans of God for that time, season, and generation. If no revelation is given to a generation, then that generation continues to walk in old structures, and the fullness of God cannot manifest for that time. We must change the Church's pattern from an organizational structure (where members attend) to the pattern of sons (who connect to the house). If not, we will never see a download of the Spirit of Revelation as manifested through His apostles and prophets.

"Having predestined us to the adoption as sons by Jesus Christ...having made known to us the mystery of His will...that the God of our Lord Jesus Christ, the Father of glory, may give you the spirit of wisdom and revelation" (Eph. 1:5,9,17). Paul speaks of the inheritance laid up for His sons, which are the dimensions of the Holy Spirit. When members continue to join and leave us at a whim, we are not bringing the Church into a place of maturity, sonship, and fullness of the Spirit dimensions available to us in Jesus Christ.

God is our Heavenly Father—the Source and Giver of all life—so, as His sons, we will see differently. The pattern of the house is not a structural organization, but a Father's house. Therefore, as a son, I sit with Him at His right hand! So, all I see and hear is from the viewpoint of the Throne, not the Cross. The Church has been trying to build at the Cross; we have songs, as great as they are, that say: "You'll find me at the Cross, down on my knees." If we are found continually at the Cross, then we are not in a prevailing position of ruling and reigning with Him! Jesus is no longer on the Cross; He has risen and is now seated at the right hand of Him, who sits on the Throne. To come to the

Throne, we had to go via the Cross, but let's not stay there. The Cross was the place of judgment where our sin was forgiven; the Throne is the place of victorious reign!

The Son of God rules and reigns seated on the Father's right hand; therefore, only sons joined with Him can rule and reign with Him. Members join our church, but remember that Heaven doesn't have members joining its ranks; it has sons who are joint heirs with the Son of the Living God! When God called Moses to the mountain, He requested the building of a tabernacle, which would be a sanctuary where priests would officiate on behalf of the people in His presence. Solomon, King David's son, proposed to build what had been in his father's heart: a habitation for the Lord. But, the temple was not made after the same pattern used by Moses. If Solomon had not allowed the Spirit of Revelation to help him download new blueprints from Heaven, then he would have kept the nation in old patterns of seeking God.

"And behold, I propose to build a house for the name of the Lord my God, as the Lord spoke to my father David, saying, 'Your son, whom I will set on your throne in your place, he shall build the house for My name'" (1 Kings 5:5). God spoke differently to Solomon; He no longer wanted to inhabit a tabernacle, but He sought after a house, which is where a family lives, a haven of deep intimate relationship, a personal habitat, and a place where father and sons dwell. The pattern in Heaven had changed, and Solomon manifested the Spirit of Revelation to download the new pattern.

Why did the pattern change? How did that effect how the temple's structure would be constructed in Solomon's day, until Christ would come and sit on the Throne of David? In those days, buildings in Assyria, Egypt, and Babylon were built with bricks and mortar. The Body of Christ has been taught to build this way; bricks represent each individual and mortar represents our relationships with each other. Sadly, we have overlooked an important key to the structure and pattern in Heaven, and that is failing to see new patterns through the Spirit of Revelation.

In First Kings 5:17, Solomon said to use *"costly stones, and hewn stones, to lay the foundation of the temple."* First Peter 2:4-5 speaks of us as *"precious, you also, as living stones, are being built up a spiritual house"* for God. Remember, the pattern from Moses to Solomon changed, and then changed once more after Jesus returned from the dead. After the resurrection, we are not building a physical building, but a spiritual one, where we are precious, chosen stones for founding God's temple.

Why did God tell Solomon to use stones *not* held together by mortar, but hewn together in a unique way so as to create a perfect fit? Bricks joined by mortar indicate a sameness of structure, design, and consistency. When we do not allow individuals to function in a personal, distinctive, original purpose, what results is a cloning of people, ministry, and function. This duplication will end up with a construction of the same building and ministry pattern. Sadly, when looking at today's Church, we can observe the successful cloning of many well-known ministers and ministries.

If mortar is used in construction, then mortar must keep the bricks together. Observing today's Church, the substance keeping the "stones" together is meetings, programs, performance, and dependency. Solomon, on the other hand, built using a system of handcrafted stones networked together by their uniqueness. Keep in mind, that when building structures with "mortar," the "structure" allows a seeming facilitation of smoothly implemented vision. But, in reality, it permits us to keep defensive walls around us that retain old truth and exclude new revelation and growth.

Religious people of Jesus' day kept structures positioned that facilitated locking in the Law and excluding Jesus Christ. Anything that prevents us from moving into current, revealed truth is a religious structure. Revealed truth must be caught in the Spirit, and then taught; this creates momentum for us to progress into, and, therefore, be established in our lives. Religious structure—or "mortar"—causes us to focus on the past, continue to look internally, and it keeps us in a place of control and manipulation. Anything that allows us to look backward is a structure not ordained by the Father. *"Blessed is the man whose strength is in You, whose heart is set on pilgrimage"* (Ps. 84:5). Pilgrimages move foreword and upward to focus on destiny.

If we are not vigilant, then old structures set in place as a relational mortar between individuals will affect the pattern, and this is what the Church will eventually build on. Such a foundation will not last, and, eventually, the building will crumble. The only means of changing structure is to dismantle it and start again with new patterns; such a process will take time and can be very confronting because it means dealing with reasons why structures were allowed to remain in the first place.

The Spirit of Revelation causes us to be built as chosen stones together, and it's also the fresh food that keeps us, preserves us, and sustains us, no matter what external circumstances push against us. Jesus said, *"My food is to do the Will of the one who sent Him."* He also said that if we eat His bread, then it is life to us. We must give people His food—His revelation. This will keep them from being harassed by the enemy. When Jesus was tempted by the devil, He told him, *"Man shall not live by bread alone, but by every word of God..."* (Luke 4:4). The "Heavenly Bread" will protect our will, mind, emotions, and physical body from the enemy's provocation.

Jesus caused furor in the legalist camp when He stated, *"I am the living bread which came down from heaven. If anyone eats of this bread, he will live forever"* (John 6:51). He was saying, "I am the *fresh* bread, not stale, yesterday's bread; therefore, partake of Me. My Words will cause you to have LIFE." How do you and I partake of this fresh bread? Through the dimension of the Spirit of Revelation!

Teachers must instruct by this dimension of the spirit, just as Jesus did. This will give people "fresh food" at the proper time.

We have been feeding people either a diet of stale bread or wrong food at the wrong time, and then wonder why we have not seen radical change! This dimension of the Spirit doesn't allow us to preach/teach a good sermon and throw out some crumbs here and there; we must become the food we are bringing! Don't just preach a message from what you are studying, but learn to come to the Father's table, take the "Bread," digest it, and then be the bread that is broken for people!

We must build the Church so that it's higher than any persecution the enemy may send. This will keep and protect the world as well. As the Church arises, so too will the world's resources and technology abound. After World War II, the Church rose and technology advanced quickly. We are about to see the next generation advance in areas of medical science and scientific discoveries to quickly overtake advancements made by the last generation.

For a download of revelation, there must be a cry and a hunger in our hearts for intimacy with our Beloved to see who He is, and *then* who we are in the Light of Him. One version of Psalm 24:6 reads, *"This is the generation like Jacob, who will latch hold of God and seek Him with all their might."* God is raising up a generation who knows how to take hold of Him and not let go!

"The Spirit of the Lord Is Upon Me Because He Has Anointed Me"

...do not cease to give thanks for you, making mention of you in my prayers: that the God of our Lord Jesus Christ, the Father of glory, may give to you the spirit of wisdom and revelation in the knowledge of Him, the eyes of your understanding being enlightened; that you may know what is the hope of His calling, what are the riches of the glory of His inheritance in the saints (Ephesians 1:16-18).

When having to present himself, Moses asked God, *"Who will I say sent me?"* God said, *"Tell them 'I Am' sent you."* When we know who He is, not only will we know who we are in Him, but our identity will be revealed to the world around us. This generation, as every generation before us, has an immense need to find its identity. The world loves to say that people are having an "identity crisis." The Church must have revelation so that each of us personally knows "who we are in Him!" Our life is hidden in God!! When the Church gets this revelation, then our identity will not be formed out of programs or conformed by world trends, but will be in in Him alone. It is not enough to get people to Heaven; we must teach them to seize Heaven and bring it to earth, so that they know who lives in them.

This generation's identity crisis is not new, but is as old as mankind. *"God said, 'Let Us make man* [mankind—male and female] *in Our image, according to Our likeness; let them have dominion…"* (Gen. 1:26). Man was created as both male and female; "he" was created in the image of the likeness of the triune Godhead. He was to have dominion over all the earth, and all that live on the earth. He was to be fruitful and to subdue and multiply.

Some scholars say that due to divine, creative order, Eve was created second, and that, therefore, Adam has total dominion and authority over her! If that is the case, and we take that theory further, then Adam is in trouble, because animals were created before him, and God cannot violate His own order! I am not saying that women are over men and should not submit, God forbid. But what I am saying is that if we understand God's order, then we will not be having this age-old discussion.

Man and woman were created to walk and function as one. Just as Father, Son, and Holy Spirit are three different people, they function and are connected as One. This is why the enemy does not want the Church to get into relationship with each other; he knows that when we walk together as one, then we manifest what Jesus prayed to His Father, *"that they may be one just as We are one"* (John 17:22). After that happens, then we will walk in divine Kingdom order, which is the most powerful pattern on the earth.

God said, *"It is not good that man should be alone"* (Gen. 2:18). He was saying that it isn't good for man to isolate, and, therefore, be sufficient in himself. This is why Jesus went to Calvary: so man would be restored in relationship and divinely connected to God the Father and to each other once again. Every time we walk away from the Body, we isolate ourselves, and, therefore, become self-sufficient!

Eve was drawn out of Adam's side, and then the Church was drawn out of the side of Christ. God presented Eve to Adam, just as Christ will one day present us as a glorious Church without spot, wrinkle, or blemish (see Eph. 5:27). Adam was beside Eve when she was tempted by a snake (see Gen. 3:1-6). Eve was taken from his side and was bone of his bone, but Adam chose to do nothing to save her. Why is that? Deception is strange; it comes cunningly, takes us off guard, and then—as soon as we are deluded—it paralyzes us into becoming passive. Adam gave into the paralysis, and, instead of fighting, he became passive and allowed Eve to speak to the serpent.

The enemy came as a serpent and spoke to Eve. What was she doing socializing with a snake when she should have been subduing the creature? The snake enticed her with his words, "Did God really say that you can't eat any fruit from every tree in the Garden? If so, Eve, then surely, He is wrong."

The Garden of Eden was not the size of your backyard; it had rivers in it, and the Bible tells us that these rivers ran through "lands," which in Hebrew means countries or nations! Why was Eve focused on the *one* tree she couldn't have out of an *enormous* selection of trees that she *could* have? She was focusing on the one forbidden fruit, instead of fruit from the mega-acres that she could partake of. At times, we do something similar: We focus on what we can't or don't have, instead of focusing on Him. The moment we focus on the wrong things, we allow our identity to be compromised and destiny stolen.

Convinced that God was holding something back from her, Eve now wanted to take control. She was deceived into believing that God was withholding His best from her, and that she really deserved to eat of this tree. How many times I have heard that story: "If God really loved me, then He would do this for me!" God is not a genie found in a bottle who is waiting to grant you three wishes!

"For God knows that in the day that you eat of it your eyes will be opened, and you will be like God" (Gen. 3:5). The fact was, however, that *she already was like God*. She was created as an exact replica—with the same DNA, chromosomes, and genes—but by allowing her focus to be on the wrong thing, she disconnected from Adam, and lost for mankind its identity and God-given, purpose-filled destiny! Eve's sin was deception, but Adam stood back and did nothing—even with human destiny hanging in the balance. It was not about what Adam was doing, but about what he was *not* doing.

Adam's disconnection from a relationship of intimacy caused him to lose generations of God-given identities, destinies, and divine order. No wonder scholars tell us that Adam was plunged into inconceivable depression! In the Garden, that loss of identity caused Adam to choose his companion over God. Perhaps this is where that feeling of "he couldn't live without her" first started. Adam now settled for worshiping a woman over God. He made Eve the center of his universe, when that position truly only belongs to God alone.

Adam was created outside of the Garden, which was a place of no restrictions or boundaries; Eve was created within Eden. When a man gets born again, he must not allow deception to cause paralysis and passivity to take over his character. Man was created to fly without limitations and restrictions, so as to break open new frontiers and create new inventions. Man was created with a pioneering spirit within him! Man was created in God's divine, creative order. Woman was created from man, and she now is able to fly with him! Adam was created with Eve inside him. Connected to Eve, they would fulfill their destiny. Woman was put inside of man to help him fulfill his future. Inside Christ was His Church, His Bride, and within the Church are future generations, and a spirit of greatness for our nations!

To understand Kingdom we must have an understanding of order. God's heart is to restore and re-establish His Kingdom through mankind, and, therefore, establish divine order. If I only try to copy a religious or performance-based pattern, I will never understand my identity in Him and, consequently, who He is in me. Many revivals have locked into the evangelist and evangelistic patterns, whereby salvation was the central point and not the Kingdom, and, therefore, they omit both the prophet and apostle! Then, we see revival dwindle out after five years. The prophet keeps fresh revelation downloaded (the blueprints of Heaven) and the apostle builds (with those same blueprints), so that we can keep the intensity of connecting to Heaven without burning out.

Jesus said, "The dimensions of the Spirit are upon Me, and I am now anointed to preach and to heal those in need." During the past years, we have stayed at the anointing level; now it's time to go beyond a person's anointing and uncover the magnitude of the Person who is the anointed One. Jesus did not want us to fix our focus on what He has, but on who He is! Father has always wanted people to receive Him, and not just what He has. After all, what father is satisfied with his sons just wanting his possessions? He hungers for their presence and company.

Father has always longed to touch earth, but if only the anointing was to touch earth, then He could have continued to maintain the priesthood. For eons of time, Father God has hungered to touch His creation physically; not Creator to creation, but for His creation to carry the divine Seed of Heaven, so His creation becomes the means that carries and births Heaven, as Heaven touches earth.

"For in Him dwells all the fullness of the Godhead bodily" (Col. 2:9). God wanted to come to earth as a physical person, not just as a visitation but to inhabit His people. God is Love; He doesn't just have love, because if He did, then He could therefore lose it! Love exists to multiply; this is the personification of love—a replica of the coming together of love, which creates a son.

Adam was not created just to enjoy fellowship with God, but to be the son whom God was going to inhabit and through him birth the Seed of Heaven onto the earth. Jesus said, *"Sacrifice and offering You did not desire, but a body You have prepared for Me"* (Heb. 10:5). God did not want the service of a priest, but the physical body of a son. Jesus gave His Father His ultimate desire: a physical body so as to touch His creation! Only a human, physical body can be the embodiment of the Godhead; a cow, horse, or dog cannot give birth to the seed of Heaven, but only a son created in the image of His Father.

When Mary said, *"Let it be done according to your word,"* she was actually saying, "Let my body carry the Seed of Heaven that will birth the body for Your Son, who, for the first time, would carry the fullness of God and dwell on the earth." For Jesus Christ, the Deity of God, to walk the earth and then leave was not enough. The Father wanted Jesus to take back from the enemy the body that Adam had given over to him, here on this earth.

Mary received the Seed of Heaven and was told that she would give birth to the King who would rule over an eternal kingdom; she would bring forth the Son of the Highest! The Seed of Heaven was a life—a Son, who breathed Heaven into the earth eternally, through the generations. God is still looking for physical bodies, for sons who will reproduce Heaven here on earth. *"I beseech you therefore, brethren, by the mercies of God, that you present your bodies a living sacrifice, holy, acceptable to God, which is your reasonable service"* (Rom. 12:1). We are the Body of Christ—His son carrying His divine seed here on this earth! We must give our bodies—just as Mary gave hers—to carry the divine Seed of Heaven in our generation.

BEHOLD THE MAIDSERVANT OF THE LORD!

LET IT BE TO ME ACCORDING TO YOUR WORD

(LUKE 1:38).

Chapter 8

The Anointed One in Their Midst

Many ministers have reduced the anointing to a sensation that comes and goes, usually by feelings. We must understand that Christ, the Son of God, is the Anointing. He is the Anointed One. He doesn't have it—for what you have, you can lose. But because He is the Anointed One, then Heaven, and Heaven's substance, is the Anointing, which is therefore Christ! The Anointing, therefore, is not a feeling but a person—Christ the Messiah, the Anointed One!

When Jesus announced "Because He has anointed Me," He was not saying "I am using the gifts of the Spirit!" Jesus didn't wait to "sense" the anointing to come on Him so He could heal someone. He was the Healer. Heaven, and all Heaven had and is, was abiding in Christ, the Anointed One. *"For as the Father raiseth up the dead, and quickeneth them; even so the Son quickeneth whom He will"* (John 5:21 KJV). Jesus, the Anointed One, operated in "the quickening anointing," which speeds up, restores, or hastens natural circumstances to bring a person into a position where God can begin to build in their life.

"On that day I will raise up the tabernacle of David, which has fallen down, and repair its damages; I will raise up its ruins, and I rebuild it as in the days of old; that they may possess the remnant of Edom, and all the Gentiles who are called by My name," says the Lord who does this thing. "Behold, the days are coming," says the Lord, "When the plowman shall overtake the

89

reaper, and the treader of grapes him who sows seed; the moun-
tains shall drip with sweet wine, and all the hills will flow with
it. I will bring back the captives of My people Israel; they shall
build the waste cities and inhabit them" (Amos 9:11-14).

This Scripture depicts the quickening anointing's function in the Body of Christ and gives us a description of the ministry of Jesus when declaring that the Lord had anointed Him. The quickening anointing accelerates faith, so we build the presence of God in our individual, corporate, and societal lives.

What is put into our souls eventually comes out of our soul in the future. If we allow wrong behavior patterns, then these will produce wrong dynamics and put our future destiny in jeopardy of being taken off course. Focusing on the future will allow us to embrace destiny. Even when sitting in a valley of dried up, decaying brittle bones, our focus must be on what they can be in the future, and not on their present status. We must allow the quickening anointing to change our circumstances into future hope and destiny.

Impartation from other men and women is a superior way of allowing the quickening anointing to be transferred into our life. This will facilitate our moving into higher dimensions of the Spirit. For many years, the Church catchphrase was "go up higher, to the next level!" As admirable as this is, if there is no one to impart a quickening anointing to us, then the process of rising becomes a slow, arduous one. Before Moses died, he laid hands on and imparted into Joshua the spirit of wisdom; this enabled Joshua to walk in the same dimensions as Moses. When Joshua spoke, all the people followed his directions without any rebellion because when they heard Joshua, it was as if they were hearing Moses.

When Paul spoke to the Corinthian church he said, "I will send you Timothy, and he will show you my ways." In other words, if you see Timothy, then all I have imparted to him will cause you to think that you are really seeing me. He sounds like me, and acts like me, because of impartation.

When I call to remembrance the genuine faith that is in you, which dwelt first in your grandmother Lois and your mother Eunice, and I am persuaded is in you also. Therefore, I remind you to stir up the gift of God which is in you through the laying on of my hands (2 Timothy 1:5-6).

What we receive from our natural family heritage is good, but what we receive through impartation is powerful. Impartation has the capability to position us much higher and adds a new dynamic that allows us to fight the enemy well.

When Paul imparted to Timothy, it was so the young man could continue into Paul's spiritual lineage. Even though Timothy had Greek roots from his natural father, now his acceptance into Paul's lineage gave him potential to pursue new spiritual dimensions. After that impartation, Timothy could rise above intimidation and stir the gift of God that was imparted to him. Paul had released into Timothy the dynamic intended for him to overcome. When a man of God imparts into us through lineage and heritage, our destinies become linked. What God has given and placed in him now becomes ours.

"Take heed to yourself and to the doctrine. Continue in them, for in doing this you will save both yourself and those who hear you" (1 Tim. 4:16). Knowing whom your primary input is, is important. Many in the Body of Christ listen to every TV evangelist, and never have one primary source (or provisional relationship) as input. Connecting to a provisional relationship connects us to the destiny of the one giving us input, and this encompasses us with a measure of protection. Connecting to a TV ministry alone cannot cover us; there is no relationship with a television set! Teaching received from a television ministry gets absorbed, not imparted. One word of caution, if there is no relating, then there is no covering! Relationship brings connection, which allows protection. Loss of relationship is how the Garden of Eden became a mess: Adam broke relationship with Eve, disconnection occurred, and of course, the rest is history!

Revelation must be given to church members to transform them from having a membership mentality into sonship mentality. Then they can be given impartation from the father of the house, so they overcome all external battles and wrong internal patterns that can hinder a walk with the Lord. The quickening anointing releases Heaven into the people and gives them a capacity to fight battles. This is life transfer. People need more than just being taught doctrines and being filled with head knowledge; there must be a transfer of a dynamic that is carried by those who are mature, so that they can walk higher in God. Moses imparted leadership into Joshua; Elijah gave a double anointing to Elisha; and, of course, Paul endowed Timothy with an apostolic anointing.

Immature people offer lots of head knowledge and usually much confusion. This is why Paul said, "Do not put a novice in an office," because he does not know enough. So, we try to solve this by sending all our immature men and women to Bible colleges. But the stature to impart and transfer into another's life only comes by maturity. We must give people dynamics to live victoriously. Many of those in church live in the world every day, and, most days, they are living in hell. Those in ministry are sheltered, so if we do not give them dynamics to live by, then we may lose them to the world!

The quickening anointing releases revelation needed for us to break through into a new level. Jesus said, *"And I will give you the keys of the kingdom of heaven"* (Matt. 16:19), and these keys are new revelation that can be transferred through impartation. When Mary spoke to Jesus in the garden, she thought He was the gardener, but as He spoke her name, His voice caused impartation. With that revelation, her eyes opened and she became the first to see the risen Lord!

Some people have been going to church for years, but are on the wrong journey. Unless they receive a key of revelation to take them into the next part of their journey, they will never walk into destiny. Without the key of revelation for the next level, they cannot go onto higher places on their journey. A quickening anointing releases the key of revelation, unleashes God's presence in our spirits, and brings us into a God encounter. Then, this breaks through the restrictive limitations and mental and emotional strongholds that cause our characters to form wrong patterns.

After Jesus' crucifixion, the men on Emmaus road were depressed, defeated, and filled with grief. This stronghold caused them to take a wrong path in their journey. As the reborn Lord spoke to them, the quickening anointing released by His words opened their eyes. Their hearts burned, which afforded them a God encounter. They walked into a new dimension of the life of Christ, had the ability to manifest His character in a new way, and came into a place of maturity, manhood, and authority in God.

The quickening anointing is given for challenge, and when it's released, all hell can break loose. What was thought hidden is unexpectedly exposed in light of the anointing! *"Now when the Philistines heard that David had been* anointed *king over all Israel, all the Philistines went up to search for David. And David heard of it and went out against them"* (1 Chron. 14:8, emphasis added).

The prophet Samuel laid hands on David and released an impartation. Samuel's anointing kept the Philistines out and placed a garrison around the territory of Israel while he was there (see 1 Sam. 7:13-14). When David received the impartation and life transfer from Samuel, the enemy recognized the anointing on David (as handed down through Samuel) and that anointing brought a challenge and fight.

In First Chronicles 14, David battled against the Philistines and defeated them at *Baal Perazim*, a name which literally meant the "Master of Breakthroughs." Here, David saw great victory, but if he had camped at this victory, then it would have become a place of complacency and not triumph! It takes one victory to gain a victory, but another to keep it! If he had not gone out and circled around the Philistines a second time, then the Philistines would have returned to take back all they lost. If you do not gain total victory in an area, then the devil returns a second time. But if the war is won, he will never obtain that area again!

We must acknowledge that a problem exists before we can challenge it! So many of us live in denial. We blame everyone else for the way we look, feel, and behave, yet never take responsibility for our own lives and actions. We wander aimlessly from church to church, always living in disputes with someone; we never confront the issue and, therefore, escape before confrontation and recognition of our wrong patterns can be resolved. Does that sound like you? It certainly sounded like me!

If we are totally honest, many of us have been around that mulberry bush, and often leave behind a trail of hurt, until one day we say, "Lord, show me what the enemy is doing in my life, and then give me courage to change those wrong internal patterns." We are to go from glory to glory—one new spiritual dimension to the next. If we are not climbing into the next dimension, but entering into a decline, then it is due to wrong internal patterns, and victory will not be gained in new areas.

The quickening anointing creates dynamics for us to persist in forward momentum; it compels our spirit into new levels of maturity, manhood, and sonship, where our spirit cries out, "Abba, Father." For the quickening anointing to be imparted to us, we need someone with spiritual stature. Today, we see young men who have been in ministry for three years who are trying to be an apostle to a man with 30 years of ministry experience. This is absurd.

Stature is a spiritual position, which is given by God through His dealings on our life as He starts to expose our wrong internal patterns and the dynamics that cause many inaccurate behavior patterns. *Status is not stature.* People in the business world have status, but only God's dealing on a life gives stature. Jacob, for example, had many promises, dreams, and visions, but stature did not come until He dealt with his character. We have to let God deal with our character, so that He marks us, just as He did Jacob.

It is not about titles, performance, or position, as these do not bestow stature. Before Moses had a stature before God and man, he first had an intimate face-to-face relationship with the Lord. When Moses returned to the place of his upbringing, he came back with stature that allowed him to free the Israelites! In times of intimate friendship, when Moses met God face-to-face, he gained stature that allowed him to stand before men's kingdoms and demonic principalities.

When we have stature, then every realm knows who we are. Just as the demons said to the sons of Sceva, "Jesus we know, Paul we know, but who are you?" It wasn't about what a famous man their father was, but rather their own stature before the kingdoms of this world. Moses affected everything that he came into contact with—be it lives and destinies of friends (Joshua) or foe (Pharaoh). Men of stature are able to break through every bondage that blocks people, bring them into a prevailing position to overcome, and sever limitations that hold back the next generation.

BUT YOU HAVE AN ANOINTING FROM THE HOLY ONE,
AND YOU KNOW ALL THINGS
(1 JOHN 2:20).

IT SHALL COME TO PASS IN THAT DAY

THAT HIS BURDEN WILL BE TAKEN AWAY

FROM YOUR SHOULDER,

AND HIS YOKE FROM YOUR NECK,

AND THE YOKE WILL BE DESTROYED

BECAUSE OF THE ANOINTING OIL

(ISAIAH 10:27).

AND JESUS INCREASED IN WISDOM AND STATURE,
AND IN FAVOR WITH GOD AND MEN
(LUKE 2:52).

Chapter 9

What Did He Say?

To preach good tidings to the poor; He has sent Me to heal the brokenhearted, to proclaim liberty to the captives, and the opening of the prison to those who are bound (Isaiah 61:1).

When reformation stirs the Church, it will transform the Body of Christ and society, and not just individuals. We have seen revivals over the years—and a measure of change in society has been experienced—but the full impact of reformation has yet to be seen. Past revivals have transformed individuals, but reformation changes entire societies. Church is a corporate being—all that happens in the Body of Christ must include the entire "Body." We see individual ministries touching and impacting areas, but true reformation will bring corporate transformation to our nation.

To Preach Good Tidings to the Poor

When Jesus stood up in the temple and read from the Book of Isaiah, He said that He had come to preach good tidings to the poor. When the Spirit of reformation manifests itself through the Church, the first result is that the Word and Spirit of grace break out in His people. This not only brings good reports to people, but changes *the state and condition of a person's life!* Grace is the unmerited favor of God, which is correct. But when grace is present, an additional dynamic comes into place.

97

Jesus was full of grace. *"And the Word became flesh and dwelt among us, and we beheld His glory, the glory as of the only begotten of the Father, full of grace and truth"* (John 1:14). The grace upon Jesus allowed the world to see the glory of His Father. The grace of God brought Him from a position of a Deity abiding in Heaven down to the earth in the position of a Son. This grace working in us brought us from a place of being His creation, and serving Him as a servant, to the positioning of a *son*.

If we continue to be sin-conscious, then we will never walk in our inheritance. Only a consciousness of grace enables us to appreciate that we are *sons*, and then walk in full provision of sonship, which is our inheritance and heritage. *"So now, brethren, I commend you to God and to the word of His grace, which is able to build you up and give you an inheritance among all those who are sanctified"* (Acts 20:32). Grace will build the Body of Christ. Ephesians talks about us being built together as a dwelling place of God in the Spirit, as built on the foundation of the apostles and prophets. This building is not connected through the substance of meetings and programs, but where each stone fits together perfectly—each hewn and handcrafted, so as to interlock together—into a building for Him, which is connected through grace not works.

The true mark of an apostle is the Word of grace. The apostles brought the Gentiles into a place of obedience and faith in God through the Word of grace. With that grace, the apostles had the ability to raise obedient sons. This grace shaped them into God's divine purpose for their life. Grace brought God's creation back to its original design. *"And with great power the apostles gave witness to the resurrection of the Lord Jesus. And great grace was upon them all"* (Acts 4:33). Grace matures us, brings us into sonship, and allows us access to our inheritance. The Word of grace grows us into a place of maturity and manhood and, therefore, gives us the ability to reproduce and multiply.

HE HAS SENT ME TO HEAL THE BROKENHEARTED

This is not merely healing the emotions of men and women—who through circumstances have been broken and hurt—but it's where the Word of God is able to restore the spirit and soul so that it's brought into a place of maturity and manhood. Those who minister "inner healing" must function in the sevenfold dimensions of the Spirit of God.

The Church has thought up many diverse theories about the reasons for and the methods of delving into a person's past. Before acting on these, however, we must remember that the only reason to deal with the past is to reconstruct a person's present and future destiny. When people are hurt, bitter, or broken, they lose the ability to dream. Dreams gone by become a vapor that seems to vanish. During tough and difficult times, people also lose the language of the Spirit—they stop speaking in tongues, which is the doorway to mysteries of the Kingdom. When the language of the Spirit gets lost, then the capacity to hear spiritually also gets lost.

The language of the Spirit is vital to our progress. Words have the power to create atmosphere, and the language of the Spirit creates an atmosphere for His Spirit. Remember, the atmosphere we build regulates the relationship and presence we walk in. The more plentiful our language, then the deeper we dig into Him. When we speak the language of the Spirit, we take out of the abundance that He has placed in our heart and download it in our natural life. Praying in the language of the Spirit gives an individual the ability to pick up a new vision, or to thrust himself into a vision once lost, and gain momentum for progress.

To Proclaim Liberty to the Captives

When the Spirit of reformation hits the Church, then people will declare the Word that can give bound people the ability to rise above oppression, sickness, and sin. If we are to declare liberty to captives being held prisoner, then we must have stature to bring release. In judicial systems, only a judge can extend imprisonment or release one who is incarcerated. The same is true in the Body of Christ; we must have a measure of stature to proclaim and declare liberty to release another.

*"Now the Lord is the Spirit; and where the Spirit of the Lord is, there is **liberty**"* (2 Cor. 3:17). When Jesus is made Lord, and His Lordship is primary in one's life, then the Spirit of the Lord releases His liberty. Some people are locked into internal prisons of fear: fears of man, failure, intimidation, insecurity, and shyness. In these areas, Jesus has yet to be made Lord, therefore, there is no internal liberty. Old internal patterns abide in the area of our soul, and this is how the enemy keeps us walking in old patterns.

Many old patterns of behavior—such as shyness, insecurity, control, and manipulation—are actually survival patterns. That was how we endured our past and managed to stay safe (or so we thought). But there is one problem: We have survived, endured, and lived to tell the tale. Often, a poverty mind-set is thought of as just a mind-set; but it's rooted in a pattern that causes poverty to be seen as a survival mechanism. Other internal patterns can be the symptom of a victim mentality; we may be ill or have signs of pain with little physiological findings. We must realize that these old patterns keep us in a place of restraint, and liberty cannot be exerted here because Jesus is not given His rightful position as Lord!

AND THE OPENING OF THE PRISON TO THOSE WHO ARE BOUND

As we said, only a judge or one with greater authority can release a prisoner before his term is served. Reformation gives us authority to cut short a prison sentence determined by the enemy. The very principle of kingdom is that a king can make decrees and laws. With a proclaimed word, these laws and edicts determine values and precepts to govern the kingdom. As we walk in greater understanding of the apostolic Church, we will begin to rise in an authority of Christ to formulate decrees that open doors of sickness, poverty, and depression.

"I will give you the keys of the kingdom of heaven, and whatever you bind on earth will be bound in heaven, and whatever you loose on earth will be loosed in heaven" (Matt. 16:19). Many Christians are

still knocking on doors in the hopes that they will open. Now is the time to walk in a new realm. Someone with a key does not need to knock; he simply uses his key and effectively opens the door! That is Kingdom mentality!

We have been praying, hearing God, and then asking Him for confirmation! This can very easily turn into a Charismatic mentality! If we know His voice, then we should simply act, and not chase a confirmation for what He has already spoken. The words we speak must become His "sent" word. His sent words have the ability to open doors for those imprisoned by the enemy. We hear people say, "I am apostolic—I have 100 churches in a village in Botswana relating to me." But that does not mean we are apostolic. Being apostolic means knowing how to use the "sent" apostolic word.

I take hold of the prophetic word and know how to release it to bring about change. If we do not understand how to impart, empower, and equip the next generation, then we cannot pass on a legacy to them. Being apostolic is all about where Christ in our life changes us from the inside out; it brings us into such a dimension that we change our generation and leave an inheritance for generations to come. Only the apostolic "sent" word will prevail through the generations. *"Heaven and earth will pass away, but My words will by no means pass away"* (Matt. 24:35).

DECLARING DECREES OF GOD'S PROGRESSIVE PURPOSE

"You will also declare a thing, and it will be established for you" (Job 22:28). Without an understanding of the power of decrees, we will not walk into the provision of authority and power afforded us on Calvary! Making a decree over our lives, families, churches, cities, and nations causes a shift in the heavens, so what is declared can now be established on the earth.

The *Webster's Dictionary* defines decree as "an official public announcement to indicate, or make known publicly, a formal authoritative order, having the force of law behind it." A decree is a legal law passed in written form, or a royal law declared, proclaimed, and made law by a king. In the Bible, men and women who released a royal decree had the power to change nations so as to release captives and bring people into divine prophetic purpose (see Esther 8:8 as an example).

Jesus prayed, *"Thy Kingdom come, on earth as it is in Heaven,"* not as a nice prayer for us to repeat by rote! This is a decree that we—as the sons of the Living God—can declare to bring about change on the earth. As we declare the purpose of Heaven, it is established on the earth.

> *For as the rain comes down, and the snow from heaven, and do not return there, but water the earth, and make it bring forth and bud, that it may give seed to the sower and bread to the eater, so shall My word be that goes forth from My mouth; it shall not return to Me void, but it shall accomplish what I please, and it shall prosper in the thing for which I sent it* (Isaiah 55:10-11).

A decree can be fulfilled instantaneously, or take the process of time, even up to generations, to come to pass!

> *These all died in faith, not having received the promises, but having seen them from afar off were assured of them, embraced them and confessed that they were strangers and pilgrims on the earth. For those who say such things declare plainly that they seek a homeland"* (Hebrews 11:13-14, emphasis added).

All these men and women of faith were holding fast to a promise. When their promise was given, they declared it into the heavens. Even though they did not see its fulfillment, the shift that took place in the heavens upon releasing the decree allowed me, you, and future generations to walk in it. Not all our prophetic words will be fulfilled by us, but some will come to pass through the generations that come after.

A performance mentality is not concerned for the sons to come, but focuses on a vision being completed by the individual so that he can receive all the glory. This is why we lose many generations, and God's prophetic purpose for mankind does not work itself out as progressively as it should. We do not pass on our God-given vision to the next generation, and, therefore, it becomes lost! Abraham's "God promise" became Isaac's "God promise" and then became Jacob's! Moses was unable to fulfill the promise of God, so he laid hands on his spiritual son, Joshua, and passed the decree onto him.

Doing so ensures that revivals aren't lost, but are progressively passed on from generation to generation! *"Write the vision and make it plain on tablets, that he may run who reads it"* (Hab. 2:2). In other words, write down the vision so your children and grandchildren can keep running with the promise given to you by God.

Jesus declared that *"I will build My church, and the gates of Hades shall not prevail against it"* (Matt. 16:18). More than 2,000 years later, we—as the Church, His Body and sons—are still walking in that declaration and establishing it progressively on the earth! We are the ones who do not allow the establishing process to be fulfilled on the earth. After a decree is given, delays, opposition, and confrontation often come. Don't give up or be discouraged. We often mistake persecution as the enemy of the Church, but this is incorrect! Compromise is the enemy of the Church today. When you make a decree, stand firm and refuse to compromise. As Gandhi once said, "Don't persecute the Church or they will grow, but [leave] them alone and they will kill each other!"

What decree has the enemy written over you, your family, your church, or your city? Perhaps, it is time to stand up and change that ungodly decree! Esther rewrote the decree made concerning her people. Declarations of sickness, poverty, oppression, and depression are all false decrees written by the enemy. Write a new one and change the legal course of your life! We must see a restoration of the apostolic and prophetic office in today's church. Prophets jump-start God's purposes and cause new decrees to be written; and then apostles establish them in God's people and download strategies for them to build with on the earth. Once we rewrite demonic decrees, then the Church of the Lord Jesus Christ will rise up and increase in its God-given stature.

"In the end, we will remember not the words of our enemies, but the silence of our friends."

—*Martin Luther King Jr. (1929-1968)*

THEREFORE IF THE SON MAKES YOU FREE,

YOU SHALL BE FREE INDEED

(JOHN 8:36).

Chapter 10

He Declared the Day
of God's Favor!

*To proclaim the acceptable year of the Lord, and the day of
vengeance of our God; to comfort all who mourn, to console
those who mourn in Zion...* (Isaiah 61:2-3).

Reformation brings the ability to break open appointed times
divinely set for God's favor to begin in our lives, cities, and
nations. The day that Martin Luther nailed his 95 Theses to the
door of Wittenberg Castle Church, he broke through that era's
religious world and released God's favor upon Germany and,
consequently, other nations.

Reformers have the ability to stand between two time
gaps—yesterday and tomorrow. Although what we had yesterday was good and effective, God wants us to transition into
what He has for tomorrow. Reformers can take people into
uncharted waters and propel them toward the finish line.
Reformers are those with the stature to stand and proclaim a
new season of God's favor. These men and women of stature
can reposition people into their God-given destiny!

After Peter had denied his beloved Christ, his life seemed
like broken pieces of dreams and hopes. When Jesus rose from
the dead, Mary ran to the tomb early, and upon entering was
stunned to find an angel in place of her treasured Lord's body.
The angel—who appeared as a young man clothed in a long
white robe—told her, *"Go tell His disciples—and Peter...."* Peter
had betrayed his Lord and now felt as if his life was deemed

worthless, and that he was no longer adequate to even be called a disciple. Now, in one sentence, a being with stature repositioned Peter into the favor of the Lord! Two words were all that was said: "and Peter." But those two words, as proclaimed to the despondent disciple, declared that this was the day of God's favor toward him.

So many people feel that their mistakes, either perceived or real, are so enormous that they have now disqualified any expectation for a future and a hope! Reformation proclaims to these individuals, and to a nation, that yesterday is past, today is a new day. This glorious new day holds the acceptable time and favor of the Lord!

A woman caught in the act of committing adultery (at that time, deserving of the penalty of death) stood naked amidst her accusers; the cold reality was that all hope for her life had gone, and all her unfulfilled dreams were never to be accomplished. A Man of stature asked, "Lady, where are all of your accusers? Nor do I accuse you, go and sin no more." In other words, He declared to a woman overwhelmed by grief and shame that this was the day of the Lord's favor on her!

Every time a believer enters into intercession, they are declaring the acceptable year of the Lord's divine favor! *"Then the Lord saw it, and it displeased Him that there was no justice. He saw that there was no man, and wondered that there was no intercessor; therefore His own arm brought salvation for Him"* (Isa. 59:15-16). In churches today, we are seeing many varied "prayer meetings" take place. Some are called the intercessory prayer group; but we must ask if there is an actual understanding of what an intercessor is? Sadly, we see much so-called intercession in our churches, including weekly prayer meetings that do not accomplish much and the women's weekly gossip time. This is what intercession is *not*! True intercession is a man or woman declaring the Lord's favor into a situation.

Intercession allows us to break through into the spirit world and use our authority to command a release for those held prisoner; in essence, we declare God's favor on an individual, group, or nation, and therefore change the natural world in which we live. The reason that the natural world is not changed is because very few function effectively as intercessors. The enemy has us chasing doctrines that he himself introduced, and, therefore, we tire ourselves out. To stand in our God-given authority, we must rise in stature and increase in wisdom.

RISING IN STATURE

"And the child Samuel grew in stature, and in favor both with the Lord and men....Now the boy Samuel ministered to the Lord before Eli. And the word of the Lord was rare in those days; there was no widespread revelation" (1 Sam. 2:26; 3:1). Looking at these verses, we can make two observations:

1. In First Samuel 3:16, Eli calls Samuel "my son." Obviously, Samuel honored the older priest Eli as a spiritual father. So, when he ministered, he did so before God and before his spiritual father! This is one reason for his growth in stature before men and God—what a powerful concept.

2. The older priest was not rising as a spiritual father in the temple! He was officiating as a priest, but his natural sons' behavior shows that Eli was not acting as a father. Although Samuel honored the older priest, it was Samuel's mother who covered him through his younger years. First Samuel 2:18-19 states that although Samuel wore a linen ephod, it was his mother who made a robe (indicative of a covering) and brought it to him every year.

When fathers of the house do not rise up in the stature as ones sent to that house, then revelation soon turns into religious rituals. Hence, we find "members" trying to find confirmation for their daily destiny, instead of hearing clearly God's revealed Word! Just because our father or pastor may have stature or a title does not give us authority to declare His favor in the face of the enemy; we must find that place of stature ourselves, through a time of God-encounter!

How many itinerant ministers scratch their heads in amazement when a pastor from the church they last visited informs them that a certain person is leaving and says that confirmation came through that particular itinerant preacher's message? The visiting minister's common response must be, "What part was that?" We need true intercessors who can declare His divine favor with stature and authority that "what is bound is now loosed." If not, we will be totally ineffective. We need to understand how a reformer spirit functions, so that we can engage in a strategic attack to defeat the enemy.

It took the birth and death of just one Man to change the world's calendar from "b.c." to "a.d."! His life was a declaration to creation itself! No wonder the earth awaits the manifestation of the sons of God! Why? Because that's when creation itself will be changed by the declaration of our life! Confusion seems to have settled in the Body of Christ as to the correct meaning of "stature." Some believe it to be status, prominence in the world, or a position that carries a title. None of these is a correct understanding of the word's scriptural meaning! Jesus not only *had* stature, but it *developed* through time and *increased* with age. *"And Jesus increased in wisdom and stature, and in favor with God and men"* (Luke 2:52).

What is stature? How do we attain it? Stature is a spiritual position, which is bestowed upon a person by God through His dealings on the personal life. It is the favor of God on our life where His presence and provision is supplied to us. Stature is not being famous or illustrious; you can be both of these and have no stature. It is not about how we "talk," but the way we "walk"! Joseph had it all—the dreams, visions, the coat, and the prophecies—but no stature, until God started to deal with his life. Joseph said, "I have learned by the things I have experienced." These experiences allowed God to deal with parts of his character and, therefore, formed for him a place of stature.

God wants to come and mark our life! Until our life wears the mark of His hand upon it, we may have position and fame, but not stature. Jesus' natural heritage did not gave Him stature; He gained that through growth and obedience in relationship with His Heavenly Father. When a person grows in stature, then he has come to a place of an intimate relationship with his Heavenly Father, which has occurred through obedience. Now, he can touch God and will invariably be able to succeed in winning the hearts of men.

Only Christians understand our titles—to the world, a church title is totally irrelevant. Moses was raised in Pharaoh's house, and after his intimate encounter with God, he was sent back to Pharaoh to free the children of Israel. Moses was able to return because he knew the etiquette needed for Pharaoh's court. If we are to affect the *kingdoms of this earth*, then we must demonstrate the life of Christ, the One who has sent us, and gain respect from the people around us.

Influence is when a person's life, reputation, and character expand to such a degree that his stature is elevated. In the kingdom or realm we live in, the people we affect must bear witness to the signs of our integrity. God said *"set a man over the congregation, who may go out before them and go in before them, who may lead them out..."* (Num. 27:16-17). Our leadership must carry accuracy in our conduct, so we lead with precision.

Honor revealed in relationships is evidence of stature—not just loyalty to a denomination or a political structure, but to the covenant of friends whom God has given to us. Jonathan and David displayed loyalty and honor in relationship to each other. We must break all limitations so as to affect one another's lives and destinies.

If a person's father (natural or spiritual) has a degree of stature, then this will enable the son to rise in stature quickly. When Moses laid hands on Joshua, the same spirit and dimension upon Moses came onto Joshua. After Moses' death—when Joshua had to stand before the people and continue the leadership—the people no longer heard Joshua when he spoke, they heard the voice of Moses (and thus, God), because Joshua had now taken on the stature of his spiritual father. When we say, "pass the baton," this is what it truly means: I pass my stature onto you! If there is no stature in our lives, then we cannot declare with authority the day of the Lord and the execution of God's vengeance to deal with powers of the enemy.

When Jesus spoke to Peter, *"Blessed are you, Simon Bar-Jonah, for flesh and blood has not revealed this to you, but My Father who is in heaven. And I also say to you that you are Peter, and on this rock I will build My church, and the gates of Hades shall not prevail against it"* (Matt. 16:17-18). The "gates" of the city is where the city elders would execute judgment. Jesus told Peter that he was being given "the keys" to the city. *"And I will give you the keys of the kingdom of heaven, and whatever you bind on earth will be bound in heaven, and whatever you loose on earth will be loosed in heaven"* (Matt. 16:19).

We the Church—the house of God, which not the building but the Body—have authority to stand at the Gate of Heaven and know to whom we should grant or deny access. *"How awesome is this place! This is none other than the house of God, and this is the gate of heaven"* (Gen. 28:17). Stature provides us with keys on earth to affect the realm of the spirit in the heavenlies.

As we arise as the Body of the Lord Jesus Christ, with the stature imparted to us, we can change the state of a person's life! Suddenly, a person's mourning is turned into great joy, and those who feel that something inside them has died are now renewed in Him. As Heaven touches them and life is breathed back into old, dried bones of lost destiny, then divine purpose once again emerges from the ashes of their lives!

BLESSED ARE THOSE WHO MOURN,

FOR THEY SHALL BE COMFORTED

(MATTHEW 5:4).

Chapter 11

A Life Resurrected
From Ashes

To console those who mourn in Zion, to give them beauty for ashes, the oil of joy for mourning, the garment of praise for the spirit of heaviness; that they may be called trees of righteousness, the planting of the Lord, that He may be glorified (Isaiah 61:3).

For reformation to transform the Church and the nation, the Body of Christ must first rise and transform the society, not just one man or woman! The Body of Christ is not an organization of separate individuals coming together to meet, but is a corporate being joined, knitted, and connected together to fulfill corporate destiny! Until the Church gets a revelation of who it is, then the Church will never reveal to the nation what it can do.

One great example of corporate destiny is when Jesus told the 12 disciples to get into the boat and go to the other side; He would meet them there. The significance of this event must be immense because it is repeated in almost all the Gospels. *"Jesus made His disciples get into the boat and go before Him to the other side"* (Matt. 14:22). Suddenly, what looked to be a peaceful night turned into a living nightmare as, out of nowhere, the sea gave way to a raging storm. *"But the boat was now in the middle of the sea, tossed by the waves, for the wind was contrary"* (Matt. 14:24).

Imagine the fear that gripped the heart of every disciple! For them to accomplish their destiny and reach the other side, "all hands had to be on deck!" At that moment, every life in that boat was in peril; six men rowed against the rampant sea and into the powerful wind; and the other six men bailed out water lapping the boat as fast as waves filled the vessel. Tension ran high and emotions were on edge in these vital minutes.

> *Now in the fourth watch of the night Jesus went to them, walking on the sea. And when the disciples saw Him walking on the sea, they were troubled saying, "It is a ghost!" And they cried out for fear. But immediately Jesus spoke to them, saying, "Be of good cheer! It is I; do not be afraid." And Peter answered Him and said "Lord, if it is You, command me to come to You on the water"* (Matthew 14:25-28, emphasis added).

The corporate destiny of these 12 men was to get in the boat and go to the other side where Jesus would meet them. But then a storm arose. When the boat looked like it was sinking, Jesus walked on water to get there. The disciples believed Him to be a ghost and cried out in fear. Jesus then calmed them by saying, "Do not be afraid; it is I!" When Jesus said, "It is I," He was saying, "It is I Am, the Creator of the universe, the Word of God!"

Then Peter replied, "If it is really You, Lord, then bid me to come." What a crazy statement! First, Jesus had just announced Himself, and second, Peter calls Him Lord! Of course, Jesus had to say "Come." He couldn't lie, and He could only answer the plea offered by Peter! How many times do we do something similar? Knowing that God has said something to us, we still say, "If that's really You, Lord, then make this work a certain way"? That is called a fleece, and all that happens is that we get "fleeced"!

Peter stepped out of the boat to walk to Jesus. He moved away from corporate destiny of 12 men to have his own personal experience with the Lord. There was Jesus walking on the water, and Peter is perhaps turning to the boys in the boat and saying, "Look, I can do this too!" This is a performance mentality, and, though often not put into words, is certainly shown by our actions. Back in the boat, five men are rowing, six men are bailing out water and one is walking toward Jesus! Are we seeing the same thing in the Church setting? When the house goes through turmoil and hard times, then all are needed to fulfill the house's destiny because it has a corporate vision. But, so often, someone splits off from corporate destiny to go off on his own!

As he cried out, "Lord, save me," Peter thought he was drowning; Jesus reached out His hand, caught him, and then put Peter back in the boat! Jesus didn't walk proudly to the other side with his water-walker, but placed him back into corporate destiny with the 12 men. Jesus scolded Peter and said, *"O you of little faith, why did you doubt?"* (Matt. 14:31) We have thought Jesus meant that he had little faith to walk on the water, but Jesus was saying, "Why, Peter did you doubt that you would get to the other side connected in destiny to your 12 friends?"

These boys were tempted and tried on the very place known to them. As fisherman, they had encountered storms before. The storm was not what brought disorientation; it was seeing Jesus coming in a different manner than He had ever done so previously. The disciples sat the boat and were merrily rowing to the other side, all while knowing the purpose of God. But their paradigm did not leave room for change!

If the Church wants to reform society, then it must stay connected in corporate destiny. When we are bound together by purpose and vision, then we keep the house's momentum progressing forward. Today, we see pastors giving prophetic words or manipulating people through spiritual gifts to connect them to the house. Not only is this wrong, but it will eventually make people leave the church and lead to offense and despair. People should connect where they sense vibrations of the Spirit calling them. When God has connected us to a house, it's to encourage and inspire others to keep moving forward and not get overwhelmed by storms that hit the house. Remember, Jesus' purpose was not to still the storm, but to keep the men rowing through the storm to destiny.

As leaders, it is important to yoke together everyone who is in the "boat." If not, we lose momentum and no longer control the speed of prophetic words given to us. The Church must learn to move forward in destiny together. Constantly looking at the negative and allowing it interpret our destiny is a symptom of immaturity. So many times, leaders focus on the negative in church and want everyone to know the negative because the negative is seen as truth!

It's true that there may be a storm, but the word sent to a church, and not our interpretation of the storm, is the true destiny of the house. We have all seen the negative, and the enemy would want us to focus on it, and thereby slow down momentum and cause instability. True maturity means to keep moving through the negative with our hearts pressing toward destiny.

"Do not be unequally yoked together with unbelievers" (2 Cor. 6:14). Of course, Paul was talking about saved and unsaved people coming together in a covenant relationship. But perhaps we could look at this Scripture in another way? *"Can two walk together, unless they are agreed"* (Amos 3:3). So, we could conclude that it's impossible for us to come together in one destiny when our thinking patterns are different. When we are not walking together, then we are not working toward a corporate purpose, which is collective destiny. Walking apart puts us in danger of being targeted by the enemy; protection only comes from a group staying together.

Corporate destiny will break open a city. But when we are segregated, the city sees a mess and not a rejoicing body. Jesus could have done all He needed to do on His own without the 12 disciples. But Jesus Himself chose to show us the nature of His Father. Jesus never once had His own agenda, but He Himself said, *"I must be about My Father's business"* (Luke 2:49). We are not created for isolation, but to be connected beings.

TO CONSOLE THOSE WHO MOURN IN ZION, TO GIVE THEM BEAUTY FOR ASHES

Reformation will restore people to full potential in Christ. We must stop looking at where people are, and instead, see where they can be and what capacity God has placed within them. Every child born has potential, but few realize it! Take the emptiness that plagues them and release them into their full potential. David was one who had been through the worst, but kept focused on the best; he took the weakest and turned them into the strongest. We must see the worst but believe the best in people.

From the heights of being anointed and destined for the throne, and after a famous victory over one of Israel's most sinister enemies, David was forced from Saul's service into life as a fugitive. Destined for greatness, his throne had become a cold, hard cave, instead of the royal seat in the king's palace. Far from palatial comforts, David found himself fighting for survival, while alone in the wilderness. Racked with endless grief, David must have felt that his life was now in a pile of ashes.

This time, the threat was not a Philistine giant, but a menace posed by David's supposed mentor and great supporter—the king of Israel himself. The Word of the Lord had come through Samuel with such clarity, and had been so obvious, that surely Saul would see that David was now the anointed successor and bow to the Lord's choice! Sadly, this was not to be. The very one David looked to for support and promotion had become his enemy. Overtaken by jealousy, Saul made several attempts on David's life, driving the young man into one of the most perplexing trials of his life.

But Saul, the leader who was "head and shoulders" above his peers, is still on the throne. (The "head" represents human thinking and the "shoulders" represent human government or control; see First Samuel 9:2.) Uneasy about this new breed of leader, Saul drives him into hiding in fear of his life. For David, the throne and his destiny is in ashes and now washed away by tears pouring from his eyes into dust on the ground. His hiding place had now become a place of delayed dreams and disappointment; he had no idea if he would ever be the person whom he was destined to be, or if he would be equipped to carry the weight of glory soon to be his.

David had been thrust out of the system—out of the old leadership and political sphere—and was now on a crash course to get that out of him. Any residue of the Saul nature in David was being exposed, so as to set him free and truly make him a man after God's heart. Every twist of his inner life was being straightened, so that he could touch God's heart and destiny for his generation. How can we be used of God except that we also be so inwardly clean? God was overseeing the circumstances of David's life to prepare him for future destiny and greatness.

Though we may be mourning in the ashes of our life in Zion, God is preparing us for the beauty and splendor that is to come. David was destined for greatness but was now sitting in ashes, as he grieved what once was and could have been. Reformation will hand people like this a garland that takes them out of fiery ashes and thrusts them into their future. *"I have seen servants on horses while princes walk on the ground like servants"* (Eccles. 10:7). We must put princes back on their horses and set them off again on their journey.

When Jacob blessed his sons at the end of his life, he remembered how their past sins had embittered him as a father. In retaliation, he reduces the boys to all their wrongdoing: *"Unstable as water, you shall not excel...Simeon and Levi are brothers; instruments of cruelty are in their dwelling place"* (Gen. 49:4-5). These are not wonderful prophetic words filled with inspiration and encouragement! Years later, Moses prophesies to Reuben and Levi. But what's different is that although Moses knew the worst in these boys, he preferred to believe the best; he lifted them out of the grief they felt from their father's final words, and the mess of ashes left of their past, to bring them into a place of joy.

THE OIL OF JOY FOR MOURNING

Reformation will bring people back from having an impacting experience to having an encounter with Christ and His presence. The Hebrew word for beauty is the word *pe'er*, which means a fancy headdress or a type of crown. In the Old Testament, people in mourning put ashes on their head to represent grief. In reformation, we will see an exchanging of ashes of grief for a crown of Joy. Leviticus 21:12 tells us that the anointing oil was to be a crown on the priests' head. The oil was to flow out of the Lord's presence and, in so doing, flow into His people. The anointing oil would then affect peoples' souls and consciousness. As they start to become God-conscious, the fear of the Lord is manifested.

We all have wrong internal patterns that we could liken to a door that keeps squeaking! We can make other noises to cover the squeaking, but the door still squeaks! The only way of stopping the door's noise is to oil it! The same is true with people. In church, we use methods to deflect our attention from the noise, but the bottom line is that the door still squeaks! If wrong internal patterns are not dealt with, then this will eventually affect the soul; soon after, a state of mourning can be sensed in the person's soul. If our past is not dealt with in an accurate manner, then our past will deal with us inaccurately. If a church allows mourning to continue—this can be anything negative entering in its midst, like gossip, sin, or wrong belief—momentum will slow down unless they are cut off.

THE GARMENT OF PRAISE FOR HEAVINESS

We must blanket people with a covering to protect them. By covering people, we give them impartation, or a power to prevail over any circumstances that come against them. In First Kings 19, Elijah was on the run from Jezebel and was feeling discouraged and depressed—even after an enormous victory. When Elijah heard the Lord's still small voice, *"he wrapped his face in his mantle and went out"* (1 Kings 19:13). The mantle was his form of protection—it represented a breakthrough spirit now covering him. When Elijah was taken up in a whirlwind, his young apprentice Elisha embraced his mantle so as to keep Elijah's life. Elijah had taught Elisha how to walk in a breakthrough spirit, and now the young man wanted to follow in Elijah's footsteps.

In the Gospels, the woman with the issue of blood was suffering after years of anguish from a condition that caused her to hemorrhage. The state had drained her of life, joy, and strength; her only hope was to touch but the hem of His garment (or take hold of His mantle), and this act caused her to breakthrough, heal physically, and return to emotional balance in life. We must teach people to carry a breakthrough spirit in life, so that no matter what confronts them, they know how to penetrate the circumstances and advance His Kingdom!

THAT THEY MAY BE CALLED TREES OF RIGHTEOUSNESS, THE PLANTING OF THE LORD, THAT HE MAY BE GLORIFIED

We must raise people of caliber, quality, character, and moral fiber, and who also have inner strength and not just outward appearance! How many times have you been passed by a speeding car or, even worse, have had a driver yell out expletives at you, only to see a huge fish symbol on the car's back window? Sometimes you wonder if he would be better off investing in an aquarium for his car, rather than advertising his inner life!

Today, there seems to be a surplus of "breakdown" believers and not "breakthrough" believers. We must build into people, so they can stand on their own two feet and not be dependent on people or programs to survive! If people are receiving correct food, accurate teaching, and good training, then they can correct wrong internal patterns affecting their behavior.

We must put Christ, and not programs and meetings, into people. Individuals must learn to develop dependency on God and not the "Church." *"My little children* [one who has an inability to reproduce] *for whom I labor in birth again until Christ* [the mature Son, who is able to reproduce Himself in another] *is formed in you..."* (Gal. 4:19). Paul knew that if Christ is not planted into people, then there is no reproduction. It is not enough to just tell people about Christ; His very nature and character must be produced, fashioned, and literally pushed out of them!

BREAKTHROUGH BELIEVERS

Most modern pastors try to change someone's behavior system—that is, a person's outlook and outward actions. But that will only change for a short time and will not establish a permanent transformation of beliefs and a core value system. Changing a person's behavior system is not enough; we must change their belief system, which is an internal dynamic that influences behavior.

In the Book of Ruth, Naomi had lost her husband and two sons. Having lost husbands and being in a place of famine, her two daughters-in-law decided to follow her. They then ventured into new territory and—having heard that the Lord had visited His people with bread—decided to find this place. Naomi tells her daughters-in-law to return to their mother's house, for they were still young enough to find a husband. Both girls decided to follow the older woman.

Not long after, Orpah kisses her mother-in-law and returns back to her former home, but Ruth cleaves to Naomi. Even though venturing to find a place of fresh bread, food, and sustenance, the lure of the old was too strong for Orpah, and she returned to a place of famine and, eventually, possible death. We can see how Orpah's belief system had not been renewed. She was still functioning out of old internal patterns. In time, these thought patterns prevented her from pushing forward into a new move.

On the other hand, Ruth had changed her belief system, which in turn affected her behavior. She verbalized what was inside, by saying, *"For wherever you go, I will go....Your people shall be my people...."* Orpah could not do this. Then what happens next is truly an amazing event. *"Now the two of them [Naomi and Ruth] went until they came to Bethlehem. And it happened, when they had come to Bethlehem, that all the city was excited because of them; and the women said 'Is this Naomi?'"* (Ruth 1:19). These two women were Kingdom women, but there was a difference: One was Kingdom-minded and the other displayed Kingdom behavior! When they entered Bethlehem, their presence caused joy to break out in the city. This is reformation!

"But she said to them, 'Do not call me Naomi; call me Mara, for the Almighty has dealt very bitterly with me. I went out full, and the Lord has brought me home again empty. Why do you call me Naomi, since the Lord has testified against me, and the Almighty has afflicted me?'" (Ruth 1:20-21) Her negative emotions, grief, anger, and mourning had now affected her belief system, which, in turn, prevented her from influencing the city! When we allow incorrect internal patterns to hide in the structure of our souls, it affects our relationships with others and hinders our effectiveness in the Kingdom.

Many times, wrong internal patterns can prevent people from thinking with clarity and also cause them to behave irrationally. People may feel condemned because they can't pursue the perceived standards. People must be trained to be efficient and successful in their undertakings; this will ensure that they find fulfillment in their quests. When wrong internal patterns control a person's behavior system, then he will seem undisciplined in certain areas; it is not the standard that is the difficulty, but the actual lifestyle. We must be aware that our standard is often very different from our agenda.

People often become religious and over-spiritual until they see spiritual meaning in everything that happens to them. To overcome this, we must train people that God moves through His appointed leaders, and to honor God, His appointed leadership, and the grace upon their lives. They must be trained to hear God's voice accurately. Usually, Christians who say that God tells them to go here and there, never establish themselves in His plan and purpose and never submit to anyone long enough to receive wise counsel.

Often, people are not willing to progress forward because of personal inadequacies, past experiences, or wrong internal patterns. These issues stop the move of God within them from gaining any momentum. They must be given strategies to overcome these obstacles so as to have a personal breakthrough. No matter what the past held, it must be put to death, so it can no longer raise its ugly head to cause defeat.

TREES OF RIGHTEOUSNESS, THE PLANTING OF THE LORD

A tree is *not* an inanimate object void of anything else to keep it alive. From the first moment of germination in the soil, the tree connects to other matter to give and partake of life. Jesus said, "I will build My church." But what He speaks of is not a building, or even a group of people meeting together with common purpose, but rather it is His Body. The Church is a living, breathing organism, with each part connected to bring life to each cell. As the process of connection occurs, we allow the Kingdom to permeate our homes, cities, and nations.

The only way to stop the Kingdom from touching us is by disconnecting from each other. All of creation is connected. Nothing exists or can survive in isolation. God made His creation to be connected. *"Therefore a man shall leave his father and mother and be joined to his wife, and they shall become one flesh"* (Gen. 2:24). "At last!" Adam cried, "She is part of my own flesh and bone! She will be called woman, because she was taken out of man."

Connection is the basis for unity, which cannot take place without connection. Unless we, like Adam, grasp the revelation that we are bone and flesh of each other's bone and flesh, we cannot expect to walk in unity as a concept. Unity is not where we come together because of agenda, but rather through a common purpose connected by destiny. God Himself is not isolated: He is Father, Son, and Holy Spirit; He is connected even within Himself. Nature itself is connected: Leaves are connected to a tree, and flowers to a stem. Fish are even connected to the water that gives life to them.

Just as a law of connection is in place for nature, God positioned a law of connection for His creation: man. His plan for mankind was for man and woman to remain connected and function as one. In Genesis 3, when Adam disconnected from his intimate relationship with God, it caused him (and all humanity) to plunge into an uncontrollable spin towards chaos and subsequent death. The moment Adam and Eve ate from the wrong tree, they severed their attachment with life itself. They started the death process by dying inwardly. Death reigned and God said to Adam, "in dying you will die," meaning that the process of death was now initiated in his body.

Death entered the earth through disconnection. To this day, the enemy knows the power of the law of connection and the power in breaking it. As there is great power and authority in connection, satan will still try to get us to work against connection rather than with it. Now, not only were Adam and Eve disconnected from their life source, but so were generations to come.

"The righteous shall flourish like a palm tree, he shall grow like a cedar in Lebanon. *Those who are planted in the house of the Lord shall flourish in the courts of our God. They shall still bear fruit in old age..."* (Ps. 92:12-14). To be planted and producing fruit means that LIFE is being produced in your life; you are connected to a system and your root system is healthy to produce fruit—not gifts, signs, and wonders—of a changed life.

When nature undergoes transformation during a change of seasons, it happens through first being connected to a life source. Being planted means that the plant gives of itself and is connected to its roots, leaves, and other parts. A plant doesn't just associate with its parts when it's in the mood. When leaves fall off in autumn, the plant doesn't throw a pity party; it stays connected to the system—no matter what. A leaf that is connected is part of the integral life force of the plant it's connected to—its future, life, and force within! This is true connection, and we cannot have change and reformation without first going through the process of connection.

"To accomplish great things we must not only act,
but also dream;
not only plan, but also believe."
—*Anatole*

Chapter 12

The Day of
Rebuilding Begins

And they shall rebuild the old ruins, they shall raise up the former desolations, and they shall repair the ruined cities, the desolations of many generations (Isaiah 61:4).

In the aftermath of September 11th—with the dust settled, the bodies removed, and grief turned to anger—there was no doubt that New York as a city, and America as nation, had no choice but to rebuild. As the rest of the world looked on and her allies forged closer bonds than ever before, America had to begin the terrifying process of finding her stability. The quandary for America was not just rebuilding a devastated city, but rebuilding its people. To assist in mourning and speed up the healing process, the solution was to rebuild trust, hope, and a state of protection, while also finding retribution for an unthinkable act.

Nations touched by terrorism and or disaster—like America, Bali, Indonesia, the Soviet Union, and now even some Asian nations—are many years later still trying to restore ruins and repair the residue of baffled, exhausted cities. This is not just an effort of external appearance, but one of internal configuration for generations to come, so as to establish a refuge of safety rather than a residence of terror and horror.

The very act of terrorism has a dynamic essence that wants to change a people's culture. If you influence culture, then you influence its belief system and core values. The seed within the act of terrorism is fear. If you can bring a society into a place of fear, then you affect its populace. Fear is bondage that locks people into a place of isolation that cuts off tomorrow's destiny and leaves them with intangible memories of the past. Terrorism's aim is to isolate nations from one another and cause allies to no longer unite together in purpose, but to become separate. It was divine purpose that the enemy's plan was foiled and we—as allies in the Western world—stood strong and united together for Christ's cause and His freedom!

Christians must stand with the boldness of the One who lives within and, like the apostles, be ones who turned the world upside-down. That was not just about getting people saved, but taking an ungodly system and turning it into a Kingdom culture—within that paradigm lies salvation. Today, as we look at embers of our past and threats that breathe fire against our cities, let's not allow a victim mentality lock us into a place of fear and spiritual paralysis. Let us dance on injustice and fight for our inheritance!

If the world fails to use these horrific moments in time as a crucible for change, then nations will still continue in their previous state of decline. On the outside, America looked to be an impenetrable fortress. Every day, when the bell sounded to open Wall Street, she stood at the forefront of those who rule the world's trade and economy. So where is the decline? Over the years, a compromise to foundational beliefs has surely weakened the protective wall surrounding the fortress of America. Enormous chinks in that armor would inevitably let in an aggressor, who achieved the ultimate disruption in peace and protection.

Could our compromise over the years have opened a door for the enemy to walk into? *"For rebellion is as the sin of witchcraft"* (1 Sam. 15:23). Perhaps the Lord is not alluding to the deception of witchcraft, but its result! Witchcraft opens up a person to the demonic realm, and the enemy's goal is to control a person. Rebellion—the Lord said *"it is as witchcraft"*—will obviously have the same result: bondage and control. If as a nation, we rebel against our leadership and disobey covenants they made before God, then how can we expect that rebellion to not have results?

Our Christian democracies were founded on the One true God, and not many gods! America was founded on the Bible as the true, ultimate support in establishing a nation, so as to form a more perfect union that instituted justice and ensured domestic tranquillity. Over the decades, that statute has become one of compromise. Some Americans have fought in the courts to have every god recognized. One woman even fought to remove prayer from school and to remove from the nation the God that education was originally established on.

Australia has become so politically correct that every "god" is recognized; Christians must be careful, as God is slowly removed from life and their beliefs get polluted in the next generation. Rebellion started to seep its way into the younger generation while the "fathers" strived for a new god called materialism. Soon, a new era was birthed with hippies and baby boomers; we gave it many names, other than its true nature of "rebellion." What had been birthed was a totally rebellious generation.

While America slept and replaced God with Mohammed, Buddha, and New Age deities, an enemy saw the crack in the door and started plotting its vengeance on an unsuspecting generation. If democracy and freedom is to fight back, then the use of guns, nuclear weapons, and men in battle array will not win this war! The only hope for true reprisal is to bring God back into the forefront of the nations!

The answer to this generation's despondency must be found in the hope of the last generation. To bring a reformation to the nation, we must lay hold of the heritage left by its early pioneers, and then build with this heritage. We must reject the heritage left by ungodly atheists, who are determined to drive once godly nations into a reprehensible doctrine of humanism. If we are not vigilant, then once again Esau will sell his birthright!

Humanism is a doctrine of hell. If we are not vigilant, the doctrine of hell will destroy the present destiny.

When sin abounds, then grace must shine through in an even greater, more superior way. An oyster is crushed to produce a precious pearl of great worth. Though America and other nations have been injured beyond compare through terrorism, they must see themselves as an oyster from which this tragedy produces a pearl of great price. *Persecution gives us the power to overcome! Persecution is not the enemy of the Church—compromise is!*

AND THEY SHALL REBUILD THE OLD RUINS

When reformation touches the Body of Christ, it will affect not only the Church, but also society and therefore nations. Reformation has a dynamic to raise a generation of effective re-builders. It's not just another "Charismatic" experience, but it is for those with genuine desire to rebuild the Church after the pattern of Heaven and allow not just for a visitation, but a habitation of God. It is impossible to have reformation without re-builders. It must be more than wanting God to come with a "new move," but should be about rebuilding His original pattern, so the "new move" has a substance and structure to be established on.

When Elijah gave the prophetic word to Ahab, he ran for his life! He soon found a place of comfort by the Brook Cherith. He drank while the city famished in drought, and ate bread and meat brought by ravens as the city starved. While Elijah was enjoying the move of God, the city was dying! God had to cause the brook to dry up so Elijah would move into his destiny, which was to bring the city into its purpose! Sometimes, we forget that cities and nations have a destiny. While the Church is enjoying its little move of God, the city outside the four walls is walking into a place of death.

Is it any wonder why moves of God have to finish? It's to get us out of a place of complacency and into a place of action! How sad that the Church still does not understand that God's move is not to lock ourselves behind a religious wall but to connect

130

with a dying company (the city) and bring it into a place of life and abundance. Elijah was told to go to the gate of the city because a dying widow had been commanded to meet him there! I can hear Elijah, "Now come on, God, I'm not sure if You realize that the old girl doesn't even have a sock to boil up and eat!" The Lord responded, "It's not about the woman, Elijah. She is just the vessel I will use to touch the city!"

In Luke 1:26-27, the Scripture reads, *"The angel Gabriel was sent by God to a city...to a virgin...of the house!"* God's presence comes to the house to find a vessel to touch the city. People who say, "I can't find a good church," or "God isn't using church today," are out of touch with God because His passion is His house! If we profess to be reformers, then our passion must to build His House.

Reformers build with permanence and destiny in mind. Meeting temporary needs is not building, but rather is assembling a temporary construction for a short period; then, it has to be dismantled after it becomes irrelevant to the next generation. A builder's mind-set is one of permanence. We must be positioned to build and establish the future on the blueprint of Heaven. If people are positioned to build, then their passion will be to construct with common purpose and destiny.

Re-builders will be so affected by the last generation's intensity that they will also have a passion to build where the previous generation left off. Samuel, who was passionate to see the ark of the covenant returned, so affected the life of David that David's fundamental vision as king of Israel was to bring the ark of God back to its homeland.

From the time Samuel was a young boy, he ministered with Eli the priest in the Holy Place of the temple. Historical records note that while David was fleeing from Saul, the future king spent ten years with Samuel. Here, David learned how to rule with a kingdom, governmental authority, but received an impartation and transfer of prophetic destiny—both personal and national. David's ability to join his heart to Samuel for eternal purpose caused spiritual progression, and that advanced God's eternal plans for the next generation and in the nation.

RAISE UP THE FORMER DESOLATION

Reformation will cause us to rebuild on the original structures created by God. As wonderful as denominations are and have been, they continue to build on structures of man and not God. They do not return to the original design but use the design fashioned by men. If we are to rebuild what was lost, then we cannot return to history to discover and rebuild it; we must return to the place of its conception and birth.

"See that you make all things according to the pattern..." (Heb. 8:5). God has a pattern in Heaven for everything He has and does on earth. One of His designs in Heaven is the pattern that Heaven itself is built on, and is named after. That is the family, as based on the order of Father and Son. To see how a father and son are to be patterned, and build and develop their relationship, all we need to do is copy the pattern already established in Heaven.

Ephesians 3:15 tells us we are named (patterned) after (or to have the authority of) the family in Heaven and earth, using the same design, order, structure, and authority. In line with that doctrine, John 5:19 states, *"I say to you, the Son can do nothing of Himself, but what He sees the Father do; for whatever He does, the Son also does in like manner."* The Father showed His Son all He was to do; Jesus then built after *the pattern of the spoken word of the Father*.

Reformers must be able to perceive and embrace insights that God is releasing to this generation, so that the Church can be prepared for tomorrow. The Church must apply Heaven's blueprint so that it becomes the design that shapes society, as opposed to the humanistic opinions flooding today's world. Society must return to the benchmark of the family as being the pattern on which our culture is built; that has been the pattern since before the world's foundation, and it must be the Church that once again redefines today's social order. If we continue building as we have done in the past—with only current trends being relevant—then we will have short succession and will become irrelevant to the future. God's eternal design is *never* irrelevant.

On Christmas Eve 1974, the City of Darwin (the capital of Australia's Northern Territory) was stunned by the touch down of a cyclone of monumental proportions—Cyclone Tracy. When Darwin was built, its design did not take into account external forces that could strike at any time. When Cyclone Tracy hit, the city was devastated. In rebuilding Darwin, if it had not restructured for the future, but built according to its original blueprint, what would have happened if catastrophe struck again?

When rebuilding Darwin after the 1974 cyclone, a great deal of structural planning was taken into account. With all traces of the city prior to the cyclone now demolished, consideration was given for its future development. Have we built the Church the same way as Darwin was originally built? Have we tried to build on remains of past moves of God, without seeking the eternal, heavenly design and structure?

At this moment, some Asian nations are poised to be rebuilt after the worst natural disaster in our lifetime. Here is our chance to prove that Isaiah 61 allows us to rebuild our nations and, in the process, reform them according to Heaven's pattern. We must have fathers in position in today's Church to help us build our lives and the "house" (the Church) for the future. How can we build if there is no one with the wisdom and knowledge to help us construct correctly?

God gave us the pattern: He said that He was the God of Abraham, Isaac, and Jacob. When three generations build with a transference of heritage and inheritance in mind, then we build according to the pattern set by God in the eternal past. Paul cried out to the Corinthian church that *"yet you do not have many fathers"* (1 Cor. 4:15), because he knew that only fathers could "build" Christ into believers, so that each one's destiny would come to pass.

133

Jesus, the Son of God, knew the pattern in the heart of His Father and, therefore, could build accurately. When Jesus asked Peter, *"Who do you say that I am?"* Peter answered, *"You are the Christ, the Son of the living God."* Jesus answered and said to him, *"...I say to you that you are Peter, and on this rock [of revelation] I will build My church..."* (Matt. 16:16-18). The Church must be built on revelation of the eternal relationship of Father and Son, for only the Father can reveal the blueprint for building. The blueprint that the Church is to be solely built upon is the revelation of who Jesus is, and not upon who men say that He is. If we try to build on who men say He is—or on men's opinions and doctrines—then the boundaries keep changing through the generations. A builder must put a structure in place for permanent support, or the building will disintegrate and collapse.

When God created the heavens and the earth, *"in the beginning* [the dateless or eternal past], *God created* [to bring into being, this work is reconstructive in nature] *the heaven and the earth....The earth was* [this word in Hebrew is hayah meaning "became"] *without form and void"* (Gen. 1:1-2), or as the Hebrew says, the earth was *tohu va bohu*, which means "waste, empty, and in chaos." Jeremiah 4:23 reads, "I beheld the earth, and indeed it was without form, and void; and the heavens, they had no light," which confirms that the earth was a waste place, empty, with no light, and in chaos.

When the Word of God and His Spirit left the earth after lucifer's sin and rebellion, the earth was void of structure. The Holy Spirit in creation gives structure. Should we omit the Spirit of God, then we neglect the very substance of God-given framework for construction of His design for the Church. When Jesus spoke to the woman at the well, He said *"...that those who worship* [have an intimate relationship and fellowship] *Him* [the foundational relationship of heaven], *must worship in spirit and truth"* (John 4:24). When we neglect the Spirit of God, we neglect the structure of Heaven. When we remove worship, we remove the Spirit of God—as you cannot have one without the other, or the end result will be chaos.

Genesis 1:2 goes on to say, *"And the Spirit of God was hovering over the face of the waters."* If the Church is to restructure, then it is imperative that it be structured on the Word of God—not legalistic systems, but on His Word alone and His Presence. If a church just structures on the Word, then we have the hard-line legalism of Word of Faith. If it structures on the Spirit alone, then we are left with a Charismatic process that leads to chaos. Neither moves are essentially wrong, but if not balanced with the Spirit and the Word, then an unbalanced structure will be assembled. The Spirit of God hovered over the earth, and the result was that God released His Word and the creative process began.

THEY SHALL REPAIR RUINED CITIES

In the period of rebuilding, we often try to find the reason behind its destruction, so as to give us some consolation or to lay blame on anyone except ourselves. This is unhealthy and will cause more problems internally than it will solve. In Joshua 6, the doors were shut in Jericho because of the sons of Israel. Their fear of impending doom had not resulted in the enemy's defeat, but led to walls being built to keep people in and an enemy out. Just because either the devil or human hands have closed a door on us, does not mean that we have made detrimental choices.

So often, Christians major on what "we" have done to cause a door to shut! However, the important issue is not *why* it was shut; the focus must remain on what needs to be done to reopen it. If we focus on the why, then our attention remains on the enemy, and we credit him with success for this closure. This breeds a mentality of the spotlight being continually on the enemy's power and not God's! This is WRONG! Just because these sons in the Book of Joshua needed a breakthrough didn't mean they were left with a future of bondage. It was up to the fathers to open the doors and let in the King of Glory!

If we continue to focus on the terrorists' deed, then the next generation will be compelled to live in fear and dread. The fathers must stand up and open the doors once again, so that foundational beliefs are not lost for this generation. The focal point for rebuilding must be centered on the city, and not the "Church." If people fix their attention on the Church, then they become introspective and plagued with myopic vision. The Body of Christ's paradigm must migrate from a Charismatic mentality (where people work for the Lord) to an apostolic mentality (where people are trained to build the city).

As reformation causes ruined cities to be rebuilt, technology gets released for Kingdom advancement. In Genesis 1:26-29, man was given authority over all things on the earth, under the earth, and even in the skies above. Every element yielded by the earth was for man to increase and use. When reformers arise with a spirit of reformation, we will see a season of amazing inventions and breakthroughs in technology for the earth to yield its sources.

It is not enough to just "trade off" what we already own, but it's time that Kingdom businessmen open new trade routes that the globe and its economy has yet to see. What we are seeing at the moment—where I swap my boat and plane for yours—is not Kingdom. But we must come to the place where Kingdom businessmen design new breakthroughs in technology that go way beyond our present concepts. If we declare ourselves to be Kingdom businessmen, then we must walk in a Kingdom conception of ideas. This means that if the Kingdom is eternal, then that's how we must see the extension of our business and its breakthroughs.

THE DESOLATIONS OF MANY GENERATIONS

Reformation restores what was lost or stolen in former generations. As that is returned to the current generation, it will not only be restored, but also multiplied on its return. Reformation will bring men and women into realignment, and will reposition and teach them to come into a new place in God already built by those ahead. In Genesis 26:15-22, Abraham dug wells in the land that he occupied. It was customary to dig wells in an unoccupied place once you inhabit it so as to claim possession. When the enemy fills up the wells, this is a hostile act that signifies a declaration of war.

Isaac inherited this land and restored the wells to the state they were in during his father's days. Just prior to this, a famine occurred in the land; Isaac sowed in the land and reaped a hundredfold return in that same year of famine. That's more proof that reformation does restore and multiply. Every generation must restore what was lost in the former generations and then bring it to a place of maturity.

When Nehemiah saw the desolation and disrepair of how the city walls had been broken down, his passion and heart's cry was to rebuild! When the city was rebuilt, he cried out, *"Did not your fathers do thus?"* (Neh. 13:18) Nehemiah's intensity was to bring back everything in the former generation's heart—reformation of the city and realignment of its people—so they would come to a place of maturity and see the city positioned to progress from the last generation.

As we saw in Chapter Three, reformation affects the lives of people, and also society in general. Revival will touch individuals and affect society and lead to having bars closed, crime lowered, and churches filled. Reformation does not just touch people, but it's where Heaven comes to earth; with that, the city receives a download of the knowledge of technology, industry, commerce, and science.

To control a nation is to remove its technology. The objective of communism and every would-be dictatorial leader is control, which can be gained by removing its technology and raping its resources; that is the very opposite of reformation. After every war, there has been an infusion of technology into nations. Post-World War II, Japan became prominent for its electronic, mechanical, mechanized, and motorized materials. Enormous discoveries in medicine occurred in the West, and space exploration sped forward in an international race. Reformation affects a city, and therefore a nation, socially, economically, politically, and culturally. When the integral structure, ideology, and philosophy of a generation are positively affected, the result is a reforming of people and society.

"Let my name stand among those who are willing to bear ridicule and reproach for the truth's sake, and so earn some right to rejoice when the victory is won."

—*Louisa May Alcott (1832-1888)*

Epilogue

The End of Part One

When God said, *"Let there be light,"* light continued through the generations, and so it is with the prophetic word of "reformation." I have endeavored to base this book upon Isaiah 61, but after getting to a few chapters, I realized that not all of Isaiah 61 could be studied and explained in one book. Therefore, I have divided it into two parts and have released this first part now with the second to come out at a later date. Should this book have blessed and/or challenged you, I urge you to read Part Two when it is released, because the ideas and concepts are not truly complete without the fullness of the rest of Isaiah 61!

In the Introduction, I stated that while I was preparing this manuscript for the publisher, a tsunami—which turned out to be the greatest natural disaster seen by the world in recent history—hit the Asian and African nations. With over 160,000 dead and many more unaccounted for, a tired, grief-stricken, worn-down government has told the nation that it would no longer continue counting bodies but just give a rough estimate.

The world now has an opportunity to use this disaster as a catalyst for change. Let us rebuild on the foundations of Christ. At this time, we must manifest Christ to the world. We are hearing, "How could a good God allow this to happen?" These are senseless arguments that will take us nowhere. But as Christ in us flows outwards and, as we position ourselves to arise, then His light shines and His glory will be seen upon us as the waters cover the sea. Then, the Word also promises that the Gentiles will come to our positioning and rising (see Isa. 60:1-3).

Western nations were founded and established on the Almighty Sovereign God and the blood of those who died to keep our liberty secure. Have we chosen to compromise the heritage that these men left us? Have we sold our own birthright? Maybe not for stew like Esau did, but surely for foreign gods! It is time our next generation knew their heritage, and that we make sure to leave them a godly inheritance, instead of an ungodly substitution in the form of humanism.

America was founded on men who had encountered reformation. They fought, and some even died, for our freedom. Having faith in their forefathers' God, they believed and taught their children that "In God we trust." England was established on that same faith in God. The very covenant (Magna Carta) written by her forefathers in 1215 declared that faith. English law was founded upon a charter established on the salvation of God! Yet, our children are no longer taught their heritage in schools! When history gets lost, then so does hope and destiny. If we do not position ourselves to take our God-given heritage, then the next generation is bound to suffer.

"And the Lord said to Abram, after Lot had separated from him: 'Lift up your eyes now and look…for all the land you see I give to you and your descendants forever'" (Gen. 13:14-15). Let's not have myopic vision and see only today but not see the prophetic promises made to our forefathers. That future belongs to generations to come, but let's position ourselves to own it as well. When Abram positioned himself naturally and spiritually, his position gave him influence to impact the earth! We will be the same; we will have what the world needs, so let our hands be full of resource. Light attracts—if we only sit in church week after week and sing yesterday's hymns, then all we are going to attract is fungus, which breeds in stagnant water.

Our positioning must start to have global impact where we become the epicenter of the nation's activity. Our positioning must cause us to rise above internal problems, frustration, and aggravation, and allow all mourning and grief to be turned into dancing! We must allow God to take this fatherless and despondent generation and turn us into a dancing generation. Perhaps, it is time that we took back our children, their inheritance, and our future. Taking our inheritance means standing up and taking back our nation and future. It's

140

time to arise and take the promise of our father Abraham. The nation is ours! Let's take it back!

Although this book has been based on the historical events of September 11, 2001, and the nation of America, please do not assume that I am speaking to only to that country. I merely used the United States as an example. In a matter of hours, that event touched every person on the planet. It is now left to writers to describe the occurrence in historical volumes, and for presidents and senators to argue the rights and wrongs of military intervention. Sadly, an incident that could have been used to bring the nations to humility, has been washed away with tears of anger, hatred, fear, and compromise.

> *Thus says the Lord: "Heaven is My throne and earth My footstool. Where is the house that you will build Me? And where is the place of My rest? For all those things My hand has made, and all those things exist," says the Lord. "But on this one will I look: on him who is poor and of a contrite spirit, and who trembles at My word"* (Isaiah 66:1-2).

When the prophet used the word *look*, he meant "to place high attention, great esteem, and regard." Or, we could also say, "The Lord is placing high attention on those of poor and contrite spirit." God is searching for those of us, and for nations, who have this spirit. These are the ones He wishes to build with and upon.

Poor does not mean lacking in natural possessions. Churches have made doctrines that disregard the true meaning of the Lord's heart. We are not talking about the poverty doctrine—more has been written on this subject than almost any other! We must have a poor spirit, or in other words, *be humble!* Jesus said the same thing. In Matthew 5:5, Jesus said, *"Blessed are the meek* [humble], *for they shall inherit the earth."*

Meekness is not weakness. It is to prefer one another, as it says in Romans 12:10, *"Be kindly affectionate to one another with brotherly love, in honor giving preference to one another."* Sadly, humility has now become a byword in the Body of Christ! Some time ago, I had lunch with a colleague who spent a few hours telling of all the reference, scientific, and political materials that he had studied. I was beginning to think that I had somehow been translated into a matrix of the past and was now dining with Albert Einstein. There was one problem: I was feeling downgraded by his successes and he was relishing and taking pride in them!

King David was a humble man. He killed a giant, went to war, sat on a throne, and knew that the Messiah (who would one day sit on His throne forever) would come from a lineage that emerged from his loins. But throughout life, David remained with a soft, passionate heart, full of humility. God rejects the proud and exalts the humble. According to traditional heritage, David's elder brother, Eliab, should have been in line for the throne. The sheep that David was caring for—although technically his father's—were, in reality, the firstborn's, and thus were Eliab's inheritance. But God rejected Eliab because of pride.

A contrite spirit is one submitted to God and those in authority at all times. To be contrite, is to obey, even when you don't understand. A contrite spirit is a person who fears the Lord and remains obedient at all costs! If we want our nations to turn, then humility must be the place we come to. Today, let us stand up and turn to the God of our forefathers and remember the statutes, judgments, laws, and covenants made before God as they established our nations.

Before she travailed, she gave birth; before her pain came, she delivered a male child. Who has heard such a thing? Who has seen such things? Shall the earth be made to give birth in one day? Or shall a nation be born at once? (Isaiah 66:7-8)

For years, we have seen the Scripture, *"If My people who are called by My name will humble themselves, and pray and seek My face...then I will hear from heaven, and will forgive their sin and heal their land"* (2 Chron. 7:14). We have thought that as long as we come to the altar, cry, wail, pray for our nation, and get up and go home, then we have done what the Word said! That's dead wrong. Humility is not an act—it's a core value, a lifestyle, and a belief system! When His people leave the building and walk with humility and integrity, then His hand will transform our land!

Let us not allow the shed blood of our forefathers—who died and were martyred in defense of beliefs that built our nations' foundation that we now take for granted—be in vain. Let us not allow the blood of the innocent victims of war and terror also to have been shed in vain.

THE VOICE OF YOUR BROTHER'S BLOOD CRIES OUT TO
ME FROM THE GROUND
(GENESIS 4:10).

Let us be perceptive enough to hear the blood of
those who have gone before as it cries out to us to
defend their cause!

ONE GENERATION SHALL PRAISE YOUR WORKS TO
ANOTHER, AND SHALL DECLARE YOUR MIGHTY ACTS
(PSALM 145:4).

May our nations be exalted, O God,
throughout the earth!

ECCLESIA REFORMANDA, SEMPER REFORMATA

References

Most of the facts in this book were taken from CNN television and their web site: www.cnn.com. In some places, the author claims literary license for the purpose of drama.

Other sources include:

* *The American Heritage Dictionary of the English Language*, 4th ed. (Houghton Mifflin, 2000).

* Carr, Caleb. *The Lessons of Terror* (New York: Random House, 2002).

* Gabriel, Mark. *Islam and Terrorism* (Lake Mary, Florida: Charisma House, 2002).

CONTACT THE AUTHOR

Wells Ministries

Amanda Wells

Address: 43/62 Coora Street

Wishart Brisbane 4122 QLD

Australia

Email: amanda@wellsministries.com

www.wellsministries.com

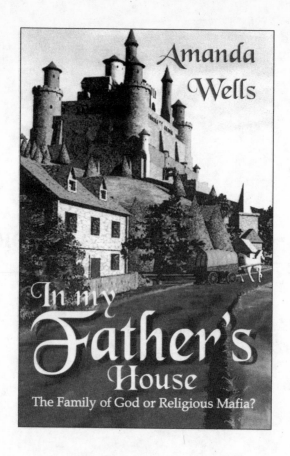

IN MY FATHER'S HOUSE

Too many men of God today are deceived into a building a pedestal, whereby, they have to keep other men from either dethroning them or climbing on board with them. This is not about pride and arrogance. Let it never become about numbers, who has more, but let this apostolic move be about lives and the shaping of men and women into their God-given call and destinies, who leave an inheritance and legacy for our sons and daughters to walk in.

ISBN: 88-900588-6-2

Books to help you grow strong in Jesus

CONFESSIONS OF A FASTING HOUSEWIFE
By Catherine Brown

This books is more than a spiritual guide to fasting—it is a practical primer on the "do's and don'ts" of fasting. Within these pages, Catherine Brown shares her experience in fasting in a 21st century world. Her humor, insight, and missteps during her sojourn will make you laugh—and empathize—with her plight as she discovers the emotional ups-and-downs of fasting. Spirituality and practically meet head-on in *Confessions of a Fasting Housewife*. Get ready to learn everything your pastor never told you about fasting! Then…fast!

ISBN:88-89127-10-4

WAIT ON THE LORD
By Lami Abayilo

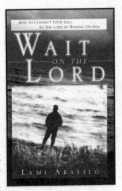

Have you been stuck in a world of containment? Are you tired of trying to find answers to life's questions? Do you want to discover the presence of God and enjoy an intimate relationship in Him? Then it is time to embark on the rich rewarding journey of waiting on the Lord. Go ahead! Unfold the pages of this wellspring of life and discover what transformation the presence of God can bring to your life. Plans will swap places. His presence will pour into you. You will know Him in a personal way. Your desires will be engulfed in the Word. All these and so much more will happen in your life because you dared to *Wait on the Lord*.

ISBN:88-89127-08-2

Additional copies of this book and other book
titles from DESTINY IMAGE EUROPE
are available at your local bookstore.

We are adding new titles every month!

To view our complete catalog on-line, visit us at:

www.eurodestinyimage.com

Send a request for a catalog to:

Via Maiella, 1
66020 S. Giovanni Teatino (Ch) - ITALY
Tel. +39 085 4716623 - Fax +39 085 4716622

* * * * * * * * * * * * * * * * * * * *

Are you an author?

Do you have a "today" God-given message?

CONTACT US

We will be happy to review your manuscript for a

possible publishing.

publisher@eurodestinyimage.com